Philosophical Critiques of Policy Analysis: Lindblom, Habermas, and the Great Society

☆

The Manning J. Dauer
Prize Winner 1988

☆

Philosophical Critiques of Policy Analysis: Lindblom, Habermas, and the Great Society

Lance deHaven-Smith

U. of ~~South Florida~~

Pol. Sci.   Unm
Florida Atlantic
Boca Raton 33431
Po Box 3091

University of Florida Press
Gainesville

Aq mig. Dir
Jim Denton

 # 16. —
$12 50

Sell discount to Book store
20 %.

Library of Congress Cataloging-in-Publication Data

DeHaven-Smith, Lance
    Philosophical Critiques of Policy Analysis : Lindblom, Habermas, and
    the Great Society / Lance deHaven-Smith.
    p.   cm.
    Bibliography: p.
    Includes index.
    ISBN 0-8130-0907-3 (alk. paper)
    1. United States—Economic policy—1961–1971. 2. United States—Economic
Policy—1981– 3. Economic assistance, Domestic—United States. 4. Poor—
United States. 5. Lindblom, Charles Edward, 1917– . 6. Habermas, Jürgen.
I. Title.
HG4936.B65 1988
338.973—dc19   88-12038
                                                              CIP

University Presses of Florida is the central agency for scholarly publishing services
of the State of Florida's university system, producing books selected for publication
by the faculty editorial committees of Florida's nine public universities: Florida
A&M University Press (Tallahassee), Florida Atlantic University Press (Boca
Raton), Florida International University Press (Miami), Florida State University
Press (Tallahassee), University of Central Florida Press (Orlando), University of
Florida Press (Gainesville), University of North Florida Press (Jacksonville), University of South Florida Press (Tampa), University of West Florida Press (Pensa-
cola).
    Orders for books published by all member presses should be addressed to Uni-
versity Presses of Florida, 15 NW 15th Street, Gainesville, FL 32603.

Contents

Tables and Figures

Tables

Figures

Preface

THIS BOOK BEGAN as a reaction to my experiences in graduate school at Ohio State University. During my years at OSU, the political science department suffered from a rift, which was common at that time throughout the discipline, between behavioralists and theorists. Although I wandered into the middle of this conflict more or less by accident because of my interest in both traditional theory and public policy, I found that I was unable to maintain any sort of intellectual integrity unless I addressed the issues dividing the two camps. Hence by roughly my second year of graduate school I had taken on the project that has culminated in this book, namely, showing how political theory can be useful in the evaluation of public policy. Little did I know then that this effort would take so long and prove so difficult.

The main impediment I experienced was my own slowness in recognizing that the subject matter of policy analysis is a theory-dependent construct rather than a bundle of self-evident actions and effects. I should have known this after reading the works of Kuhn, Feyerabend, Toulmin, and others in the philosophy of science, but I was misled by my education in the methodology of policy research. The standard approach to policy analysis rests implicitly on a military model which has been inappropriately applied to the evaluation of social programs. Policy analysts speak of "target groups," "delivery systems," and "impacts" because much of their methodology was developed during the 1960s for use in choosing between alternative weapons systems. However, policy and the effects of policy are not obvious things which leap out to the quantifying observer like airplanes, bomb craters, and bodies. Policy is better conceived as a multifaceted effort to mitigate complicated social problems, the causes of which are subject to dispute, than as some sort of projectile aimed at a "target" population.

As straightforward as this conclusion now seems to me, I reached it only through fits and starts as I tried to develop a political-theoretical methodology for policy analysis. I began, in my dissertation at OSU, with the position that narrowly focused policy research could provide crucial tests for choosing between conflicting political theories. In certain respects, this premise proved fruitful. Using the theories developed by Charles Lindblom in *Politics and Markets* and Jürgen Habermas in *Legitimation Crisis,* I analyzed a small employment program for Vietnam-era veterans and found that the theories led me to consider potential program impacts that I would have overlooked if I had used the standard, atheoretical methodology of policy analysis.

However, despite the value of the dissertation as a learning experience, the methodology it proposed did not really satisfy me, for two reasons. First, I was troubled by the argument made in the policy literature that social and political theory are politically impractical. The literature claimed that policy evolves incrementally as programs are adjusted to correct obvious problems, and yet the analytic approach that I was advocating addressed questions about the overall design of the political-economic system.

Second, I suspected that the methodology could not produce evidence to support an informed choice between conflicting political theories. Although at this point I did not fully understand the difficulty of the task, I was certain that the methodology proposed in the dissertation did not go far enough. The presupposition was that findings from a single program could serve as the basis for conclusions about perennial issues in political theory. This, though, failed to resolve how to deal with the normal pattern in policy research (and science) of having observations from a multitude of projects. Can pluralism or critical theory be seriously challenged by the results of a single program? Probably not. If, then, many instances or tests are required, how are we to tally the score when judging conflicting theories?

To deal with these weaknesses in the methodology, I decided to analyze policy at a different level. Rather than limiting the research to individual programs, I proposed analyzing "policy frameworks" such as the New Deal, the Great Society, and the Reagan Revolution. This position was presented in a paper co-authored by Randall B. Ripley (deHaven-Smith and Ripley, 1984).

The shift from individual programs to policy frameworks addressed my concerns about political practicality by changing the research audience. The narrow focus of most policy analysis presupposes that our audience is mid-level legislators and program administrators, but it is not at all clear that this is who we should be advising. My own view is that the political process includes a number of groups who affect policy—notably the electorate, organized interests, and top leaders in government. Political theory may not be particularly relevant to mid-level legislators and bureaucrats, but it has a great deal to say to these other groups.

With respect to my methodological concerns, a focus on policy frameworks helped in the effort to choose between conflicting theories by allowing me to consider the overall weight of the evidence rather than isolated findings. This approach itself would turn out to have problems, but it was an improvement over my initial position, which focused on individual programs. A weight-of-the-evidence strategy required that a domain of inquiry be delineated that, while larger than a single program, was nevertheless limited. Otherwise, the weight of the evidence at any given time was always open to the addition of new facts that might tip the scales in a different direction. The policy frameworks discussed in everyday politics limited the range of programs to be evaluated so that closure was possible in efforts to assess contending theories.

I did not realize the problems entailed by this approach until, in the early stages of writing this book, I began analyzing the Great Society. All along, I had been clinging to empiricist presuppositions that I now believe are highly questionable. My initial approach, which focused on a single program, sought theoretical import by identifying points of disagreement between theories and using policy impacts as a "critical test." Broadening the domain of inquiry to include all of the evidence from a given policy framework simply applied a "critical test" model to multiple programs. By the "weight of the evidence" I meant which of two conflicting political theories was correct most often in those instances where the theories implied contradictory, or at least dissimilar, hypotheses. But—and here is the problem—if the object-domain is distilled down to include only those points where the theories touch or overlap, the most interesting findings will often be left out. One theory will bring to light one set of findings, and another theory will unearth an entirely different set, but the evidence pertinent to their theoretical disputes will be minimal.

At this point I shifted to my current position. I now believe that political theories give us templates for identifying society-wide "impacts" that extend far beyond program participants. Efforts to choose between theories, while important because they stimulate debate, will always be tentative because theories can be reformulated, the importance attached to different public problems can shift, and evidence can be added or reinterpreted. Realistic objectives for policy analysis are to be cognizant of theoretical issues and to target research where it will be most fruitful at any given time.

I appreciate very much the comments and suggestions I received as I worked on the manuscript. Special thanks go to five colleagues: Randall B. Ripley of Ohio State University, Robert J. Huckshorn of Florida Atlantic University, Charles E. Lindblom of Yale University, Richard Weiner of the University of North Florida, and an anonymous reviewer for the University of Florida Press. In particular, Professor Weiner provided invaluable advice on how I should present my argument, and without him I could not have gotten the book into its final form. I would also like to thank Linda Adams and Ann Cannon for their work in typing the manuscript and helping prepare it for publication. Finally, I am grateful to the staff of the University of Florida Press, whose encouragement sustained me through some difficult times in the publication process.

Chapter 1
Problems of Analysis in the Great Society

POLICY SCIENCES, championed three decades ago by Harold Lasswell (1951) to study changes in the institutional order, are now an accomplished fact, but not in anything near the form that Lasswell envisaged. Most policy research focuses on individual programs and simply assesses whether they achieve policy makers' narrow programmatic objectives.[1] Approaches grounded in comprehensive social and political theory have been rejected because they are supposed to address issues of little interest to legislators and administrators (Truman, 1968; Gans, 1971; Coleman, 1972; Ravenal, 1974).

This book is an attempt to show that policy analysts made a serious mistake when they omitted comprehensive theory from their enterprise. My thesis is that policy analysis without broad, philosophical frames of reference is blind to the most important policy impacts. I make this argument by examining the Great Society from four different perspectives: the cultural theory of poverty on which the Great Society was based; the welfare dependency and supply side theories of the Reagan administration; the pluralist theory of Charles Lindblom; and the critical theory of Jürgen Habermas.[2] My aim in beginning with interpretations found in national politics and then moving to analyses developed from comprehensive social and political theories is to show that abstract philosophical perspectives provide insights about public policy that narrower viewpoints overlook.

I selected the Great Society as the topic of analysis because to this day it remains controversial. Charles Murray (1984) has written recently that antipoverty programs were self-defeating because, in effect, they paid people to be poor. John Schwarz (1983), on the other hand, says that the Great Society is "America's hidden success" in dealing with social problems. These same conflicting perspectives are also evident in debates surrounding the Reagan Revolution, which dismantled many of the programs established in the 1960s and '70s. Supporters of the Reagan policies see Great Society programs as impediments to the economic prosperity which in their view is the only real solution to poverty; opponents of the Reagan Revolution claim that antipoverty programs are needed to maintain equality of opportunity and assure that the benefits of the economy are shared by everyone (Palmer and Sawhill, 1982).

The Same Facts, Different Conclusions

For policy analysts, the failure to resolve this debate over the Great Society should be very puzzling. Because it coincided with the emergence of policy analysis, the Great Society was studied more thoroughly than any other set of policies in history. Individual programs were evaluated with rigorous methodologies, large-scale experiments were conducted on a variety of alternative approaches to the problem of poverty, and the level and distribution of poverty were tracked carefully over time. In some instances, more money was spent on research than on the programs being examined. Given the vast body of information developed from policy research, why does this disagreement over the Great Society persist?

Although other explanations are possible (cf. Aaron, 1978; Nathan, 1986), in my view the disagreement continues principally because the findings provided by policy research are too crude and atheoretical to resolve the issues in question. Evidence from narrowly focused research on program performance is indecisive in political debates because it can be, and is, interpreted in many different ways.

Consider the debate over income transfers and social services. There is almost complete agreement on the evidence, and yet welfare is one of the central issues over which defenders and critics of the Great Society are divided.

No one disputes that welfare undermines work motives among at least a part of the labor force, but liberals and conservatives interpret this fact quite differently. Schwarz (1983, p. 40) says that it is a small problem because the disincentive is limited to a very narrow segment of the population: "it is most likely to be experienced by those Americans who remain at or near the poverty level even when holding down full-time jobs." For Murray (1984, pp. 184–85), on the other hand, welfare's work disincentives are of overriding importance *precisely because* they are concentrated on the working poor:

> One may approve or disapprove of Food Stamps and Medicaid and housing assistance, but one result was inevitable. . . .
> Pride in independence was compromised, and with it a certain degree of pressure on the younger generation to make good on the family tradition.
> More importantly, working people who made little money lost the one thing that enabled them to claim social status. For the first time in American history, it became socially acceptable within poor communities to be unemployed, because working families too were receiving welfare.

Hence, whereas Schwarz says that welfare helped millions of people, Murray concludes that it destroyed "status rewards" for the working class and, ultimately, the work ethic of new generations.

The conflict between these perspectives is also immune to data on the duration of welfare participation, specifically in Aid to Families with Dependent Children (AFDC). Just as he discounted the problem of work disincentives, Schwarz (1983, p. 42) sees the problem of welfare dependency as minor.

> Critics contend that long-term welfare dependency frequently develops in [welfare] families. However, AFDC actually experiences a very high turnover. One study reports that 75 percent of all AFDC cases close within three years; another puts the figure at 60 percent.

Gilder (1981, p. 150), one of the intellectual architects of the Reagan Revolution, agrees with Schwarz's observation, but he casts it in a different light:

> As serious as existing welfare problems may seem, they are dwarfed by the potential crisis. At present, even among the actual AFDC clients, only one-fifth have actually capitulated to the entire syndrome of the welfare culture. Only 20 percent accept the dole as a more or less permanent way of life. That 20 percent, though, takes 60 percent of the money.

Thus for Schwarz the turnover in AFDC is a source of consolation, but for Gilder it means that the problem of "welfare dependency" may become overwhelming. Like optimists and pessimists looking at the same proverbial glass of water, they reach very different conclusions.

Even the so-called feminization of poverty cannot resolve the welfare issue. Over the past fifteen years, poverty has become increasingly concentrated among households headed by females.[3] For welfare's defenders, this means that income supports and social services are needed now more than ever, because female heads of households, particularly those with young children, cannot be expected to earn enough to support their families. "Simply put," say Bawden and Palmer of the Urban Institute (1984, p. 198), "the problem is that a growing majority of the poor are in households that benefit little from economic growth." However, Murray asks (1984, p. 32):

> What are causes and what are effects? Did reductions in poverty create a new profile of the poor (in effect, weeding out the two-parent families), or did poor people start to behave differently with regard to marriage and divorce? *Why not BOTH?*

In Murray's view welfare caused the feminization of poverty by undermining the recipients' family structure, and hence he advocates the elimination of welfare rather than its continuation or expansion.

In short, the facts on program performance do not speak for themselves. Those who base their arguments on findings about the short-term impacts of government programs quickly become victims of misplaced certitude. The findings from most research on public policy admit of many interpretations, and partisan analyses like those of Schwarz, Murray, Gilder, and others stand on shifting ground.

Framing the Possibilities

When evaluating public policies, analysts inevitably place the facts in a context of alternative possibilities. We can see this quite clearly in the debate over income and in-kind transfers. For a defender of welfare, it is impossible to have a society with acceptable jobs for everyone. In Schwarz's words (1983, p. 39):

> The government's [welfare] programs were vital in fighting poverty because the private sector was itself incapable of making more than a marginal dent in poverty among the millions of Americans who remained trapped with the weaker economic groups, either too old to get work or channeled into dead-end jobs that often paid little more than half-time wages for full-time work.

For the opponents of welfare, precisely the opposite is true: it is impossible to provide significant amounts of welfare without doing more harm than good. In Gilder's words (1981, pp. 147–48):

> Any welfare system will extend and perpetuate poverty if its benefits exceed prevailing wages and productivity levels in poor communities. As long as welfare is preferable (as a combination of money, leisure, and services) to what can be earned by a male provider, the system will tend to deter work and undermine families.

Liberals and conservatives do not disagree about the effects of welfare on work motives, the amount of turnover in AFDC, or the feminization of poverty. They disagree about the possible ways in which poverty can be handled, and this disagreement shapes their interpretation of the facts.

The same principle applies to evaluations of the Great Society as a whole. The issues dividing the Great Society's critics and defenders center on the various forms of society that are considered to be possible or achievable. The policy framework itself was premised on a theory that looks at policy from a historical perspective and points to a future where poverty will have been eliminated. In contrast, the theory guiding the Reagan Revolution focuses on existing, modern industrial societies and concludes that a certain amount of poverty is inevitable. These conflicting conceptions of the sociopolitical possibilities are based on different views of human nature and lead to different conclusions about political strategy, the proper role of government, and the appropriate criteria for interpreting the Great Society's results.

The Historical Perspective

The historical perspective underlying the Great Society was implicit in President Johnson's speech to Congress announcing his new initiative (quoted in Levitan and Taggart, 1976, p. 3):

> We stand at the edge of the greatest era in the life of any nation. For the first time in world history, we have the abundance and the ability to free every man from hopeless want, and to free every person to find fulfillment in the works of his mind or the labor of his hands.
>
> Even the greatest of all past civilizations existed on the exploitation of the misery of the many.
>
> This nation, this people, this generation, has man's first chance to create a Great Society.

In this call to action, President Johnson has divided history crudely into the past, the present, and the future. The present differs from the past in having "the abundance and the ability to free every man from hopeless want," and the future that beckons differs from the present in offering every person the opportunity "to find fulfillment in the works of his mind or the labor of his hands."

Underlying this image of history is a conception of human nature and culture. As we shall see in more detail in the next chapter, the Great Society assumed that the poor are trapped within a pathological "culture of poverty," an ambitionless culture developed in response to misery and limited opportunities. The unstated corollary of this thesis is that the rest of the public has a culture characterized by achievement orientations and commitments to democratic norms. The intent of the Great Society was to remove the poor from their misery so that they would adopt the culture of the larger society and join the economic, educational, and political competition.

This premise that the society has a stable and enduring (albeit in some instances not fully distributed) culture has implications for practical politics, substantive policy, and policy evaluation. With respect to politics, it leads to a strategy of reminding the public of the nation's ideals. When reading the 1964 *Economic Report of the President* (hereafter cited as *ERP*), which presented the theoretical foundations of the Great Society, one is struck by its moralistic tone (p. 78):

> The nation's attack on poverty must be based on a change in national attitude. We must open our minds and eyes to the poverty in our midst. Poverty is not the inevitable fate of any man. The condition can be eradicated; and since it can be, it must be. It is time to renew our faith in the worth and capacity of all human beings; to recognize that, whatever their past history or present conditions, all kinds of Americans can contribute to their country; and to allow Government to assume its responsibility for action and leadership in promoting the general welfare.

The purpose of this moralistic appeal was to generate "an aroused public conscience" (*ERP*, 1964, p. 77). Government was seen as responsible "for action and leadership" in renewing "our faith in the

worth and capacity of all human beings." To address the culture of
poverty, the culture of the nation had to be mobilized.

The theory's policy implications concern the relationship between politics and economics. The assumption that the nation has a
culture that is independent of politics and that can be counted on
when trying to mobilize support for new initiatives is also part and
parcel of the Great Society's premise that government can intervene
in the economy without disrupting economic activity. The Great Society assumed that government could function as a sort of econo-
mist writ large, as a technician who adapts the labor force to available jobs and stimulates consumer purchasing power. Welfare could
be expanded without undermining the work motives of the general
population because, supposedly, most workers have a work ethic
that does not yield to small economic incentives.

The implication for policy analysis is that the impacts of antipoverty programs will not extend beyond the poverty population at
which they are aimed. The central questions for research are, did the
government's resources reach the poor, did the culture of the poor
become more achievement oriented, and, if so, did the poor benefit
from their increased effort. Again, the assumption is that, because
of their relatively pleasant situation and wide-ranging opportunities,
the middle and upper classes have a stable culture oriented toward
upward mobility. In theory, this dominant culture would not be affected by modest programs aimed at helping the poor.

The Comparative Perspective

The alternative approach used by the Reagan administration
of framing the political and economic possibilities by comparing
different types of modern industrial societies is evident in the 1982
Economic Report of the President (p. 27):

> Political freedom and economic freedom are closely related. Any
> comparison among contemporary nations . . . demonstrates two
> important relationships between the nature of the political system
> and the nature of the economic system:

- All nations which have broad-based representative government and civil liberties have most of their economic activity
organized by the market. *true but trivial: within OECD market economies*
  - Economic conditions in market economies are generally
superior to those nations (with a comparable culture and a comparable resource base) in which the government has the dominant economic role. *US vs BRD: which has higher wages*

In this brief analysis, modern industrial societies are classified according to whether or not they have most of their economic activity
"organized by the market." Those that do are said to have "generally superior" economic conditions and "broad-based representative government and civil liberties." Presumably, those societies
whose economic activity is centrally directed have poorly functioning economies and repressive, undemocratic governments.

The belief that government intervention in the economy has
major effects on economics and politics is based on an economic
conception of human nature which leaves little room for notions of
cultural development or inertia. People are thought of as driven by
economic incentives and disincentives. This view is stated clearly
in the thesis that the poor manipulate the welfare system to maximize their benefits and avoid work.

As with the historical theory of the Great Society, the comparative theory of the Reagan Revolution has practical, substantive, and
analytical implications. The practical implication is that policy
makers must appeal, not to the public conscience, but to the electorate's economic rationality. When Ronald Reagan was debating
President Carter during the 1980 presidential campaign, he did not
rely on the electorate's potential concerns about the poor; rather, he
pointed to voters' personal, economic situation. "Are you better off
today," he asked, "than you were four years ago?" Similarly, once
in office President Reagan sought to develop public support for his
budget cuts by making a slew of cuts all at once and packaging
them with tax reductions. This strategy assumed that voters would
be assessing how the overall budget affected them personally in
economic terms. As the 1982 *Economic Report of the President* ex-

plained (p. 46): "If enough cuts can be made simultaneously, most individuals may recognize that, while they may lose from cuts in a specific program, they gain enough from cuts in other programs and in lower taxes to compensate for their losses."

The substantive implication of an economic conception of human nature is that government intervention into the economy will be counterproductive. In theory, efforts to adjust the economy's performance by stimulating consumer demand will not work because the public does not have a set of habits and goals that are firm and enduring. To the contrary, the public will anticipate future policies and change its behavior, thus making efforts to fine-tune the economy backfire. This premise was the basis in part for the Reagan administration's explanation of stagflation: "Stop and go" fiscal and monetary policies produce "inflationary expectations." Consistency and stability are required for policy to be effective.

In analyzing the Great Society, this theory shifts the focus from the poor to the near poor. The hypothesis is that everyone is motivated by economic incentives and trade-offs. If this is true, welfare and social programs will entice the working poor to quit their jobs, because, given their low earnings, these individuals will experience a net gain in income and leisure by becoming eligible for government transfers. Moreover, as taxes are increased to pay for the expansion in welfare necessitated by the withdrawal of the near poor from the labor force, incentives and disincentives will shift and additional people will be attracted to enter poverty. If the process is allowed to continue indefinitely, welfare could destroy the entire social order. Thus, from this perspective the central question for research is what effect did the Great Society's programs have on the work orientations of people just above the poverty line.

At this point, we can begin to see why data from policy research on program performance does not resolve the debate over the Great Society: different theories provide different criteria for selecting and interpreting the evidence. Conservatives believe that the behavior of workers and employers changes rapidly in response to market incentives. Consequently, in evaluating the Great Society they zoom in on income and in-kind transfers and their effects on labor force entry. That welfare undermined work motives is for them the single most important fact about the Great Society, a fact that stands out from all the other findings. Liberals, on the other hand, believe that we are entering a new age which has the abundance to provide a fulfilling life for everyone. For them the question of relevance is not whether social programs undermined work motives, but whether and to what extent social programs alleviated deprivation. Hence, in their analysis the work disincentives of welfare are shifted to the background and the reductions in poverty associated with income transfers move to center stage. When liberals and conservatives look at the data on program performance, they literally see different things.

data alone not sufficient

Theory-Based Approaches to Policy Analysis

The conclusion we have just reached is not surprising. Many scholars have critiqued the prevailing methodology of policy research by showing that it is insensitive to theoretical issues (for example, see MacRae, 1971; Tribe, 1972; Lowi, 1973; Feldman, 1976; Anderson, 1979). The real difficulty resides not in explicating the theoretical origins of disputes over public policy but in devising an approach to policy research that offers hope for resolving the issues thus uncovered. In the chapters ahead, several proposed strategies will be examined.

One idea for bringing theoretical questions into policy analysis is to treat programs as if they were tests of policy makers' theories or unstated assumptions. This strategy can be traced to Karl Popper, who argued in *The Open Society and Its Enemies* (1966; first published in 1944) that workaday government activities are actually "piecemeal social experiments." Popper urged social scientists and politicians to use these experiments as an opportunity to develop "an empirical social technology" (pp. 162–63, 291). Today this viewpoint is probably the dominant position of academics in the field of policy studies. It is advocated by such luminaries as Donald T. Campbell and Julian C. Stanley (1963), Randall B. Ripley

(1977), and Richard Nathan (1986). The theory-testing model of policy research involves explicating policy makers' assumptions about the problems they are trying to solve, developing hypotheses about program impacts that would be expected on the basis of these assumptions, and then conducting research to see if the predicted impacts occur.

In the next chapter we shall apply this approach to the Great Society and find that it has a serious inadequacy. Specifically, in cases where programs or sets of programs fail to produce their expected impacts, findings from the theory-testing model can always be explained away—as due not to faulty theory but to inadequate funding, poor implementation, improper research, or any number of factors. Thus, an approach that aims at testing policy premises offers little hope for resolving political disputes.

A second proposal is to treat programs as social experiments not for testing just one theory but for choosing between two or more *conflicting* theories. Recognizing that analysts with different perspectives will evaluate the same program in different ways, advocates of this theory-comparison approach see policy research as a means for bringing clashing viewpoints into contact with each other and resolving the conflict with evidence. For example, Alice Rivlin (1974, p. 1) has encouraged policy analysts to assess alternative premises about the "type of activity the central government should undertake"—what she calls "policy strategies." In a somewhat different vein, Peter G. Brown (1976) has advocated examining programs from a variety of partisan perspectives to assure that different points of view are covered.

We shall try this strategy in chapter 3 and find that it, too, has serious weaknesses. One problem is the difficulty, if not impossibility, of designing research that yields definitive results vis-à-vis conflicting theories. Evidence is always subject to interpretation, and the fact that multiple theories are involved only complicates the matter. Second, even if this first problem is overcome, there remains the possibility that the issues found in politics may themselves be too limited. Despite their many disagreements, advocates of the Reagan Revolution and defenders of the Great Society agree in endorsing the main elements of America's political and economic system, and yet it is certainly possible that the accepted objectives of public policy cannot be achieved without fundamental revisions to the nation's institutions. In short, a strategy of designing research to choose between the conflicting theories found in national politics is open to the charge of having limited vision.

This consideration has led to a third proposal. Although it has not yet been developed in detail, the general idea is to design policy research to evaluate political ideologies and political-economic systems. For example, Sjoberg (1975) advocates developing a "countersystems analysis" where the existing social order is contrasted with a "utopian model" so that researchers can transcend "the inherent tensions between the advantaged and the disadvantaged." Similarly, Fischer (1980, p. 194) says that policy analysts must assess "ideological systems" because such systems sometimes "produce policies that are politically acceptable but fail to work." Likewise, Jantsch (1970) calls for analysts to forecast the futures that will follow from different institutional arrangements. He seems to have in mind a futurology linked to current political issues.

I believe that the strategy suggested by Sjoberg, Fischer, and Jantsch is on the right track, but two problems must be overcome for it to be workable. First, methods must be developed for determining what types of political-economic systems are possible and which ones would best achieve our shared values. Otherwise, countersystems analysis, ideological critique, and political futurology rest largely, if not entirely, on the particular preferences of the analyst. The second area where more thought is needed involves political practicality. Philosophers and social theorists interested in policy research have not yet shown that they have something to offer to citizens and policy makers dealing with mundane problems.

My own view is that both of these problems can be solved simultaneously by introducing critical theory and pluralism into the analytical enterprise. In chapters 4 through 7 we shall explore the different ways in which Lindblom and Habermas lead us to evaluate the Great Society. They identify factors that in theory can be manipulated to move through a spectrum of alternative forms of social organization (fig. 1-1). Each of their conceptions of the societal possibilities is like a transparency that can be superimposed on American politics to locate crucial aspects of public policy and trace their effects on the overall society. It is in this latter capacity that the theories offer important new insights and also validate, or fail to validate, their premises. The persuasiveness of each theory depends not so much on its being able to withstand empirical testing but on its ability to show us impacts from the Great Society that otherwise we would have failed to see.

Lindblom argues that the key to altering the scope and nature of public problems is "politico-economic mechanisms," that is, property rights and constitutional rules that determine the strength of government relative to the private sector. In his view, a minor change in politico-economic mechanisms will cause major changes in politics and culture. From this perspective, the most important programs of the Great Society were civil rights laws that altered the balance between government and business. Lindblom's theory allows us to see that the impacts of these programs extended far beyond the groups they were designed to benefit. Not only did civil rights laws expand the employment opportunities and political participation of racial and ethnic minorities; they altered the terms of discourse in American politics, led to the political mobilization of women, homosexuals, senior citizens, and other groups experiencing discrimination, and had profound, positive effects on the public's tolerance of racial and social differences.

Whereas Lindblom directs our attention to the effects of the Great Society on the public's political demands, Habermas turns our focus to the conditions surrounding the policy framework's formulation and evolution. Habermas argues that the driving force in history is an expectation, built into the nature of language, that norms, laws, and institutions will serve the interests of the entire population and not just those of a special group. In his view, policy makers in capitalist societies are having to fend off this expectation by simultaneously correcting some of the inequities of the market, denying that they have control over people's economic circumstances, and defending the market as an equitable allocator of in-

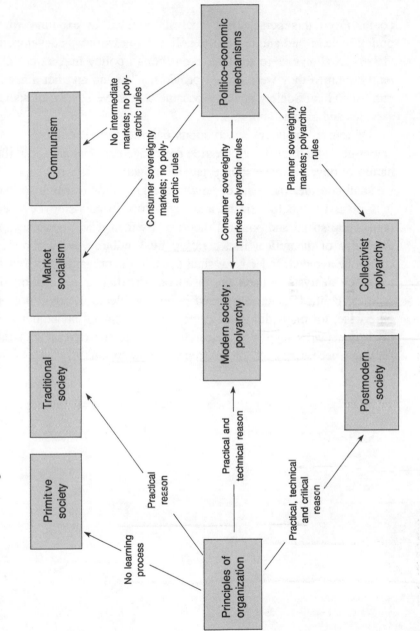

Figure 1-1. Alternative Forms of Society Delineated by Lindblom and Habermas

Politico-economic mechanisms

No intermediate markets; no polyarchic rules → Communism

Consumer sovereignty markets; no polyarchic rules → Market socialism

Consumer sovereignty markets; polyarchic rules → Modern society; polyarchy

Planner sovereignty markets; polyarchic rules → Collectivist polyarchy

No learning process → Primitive society

Practical reason → Traditional society

Practical and technical reason → Modern society; polyarchy

Practical, technical and critical reason → Postmodern society

Principles of organization

come. From this perspective, analysts are led to examine what policy makers said and did as the policy framework was developed. Habermas allows us to see that, even though policy makers consistently claimed they were simply providing "a hand and not a handout," the Great Society actually became a massive system of social services and income supports.

Of course, the novel observations derived from Lindblom's and Habermas's theories do not provide definitive conclusions about the nature of poverty or the appropriate antipoverty policy. In chapter 8 we shall consider the issue of how to design policy research so that it is of assistance to citizens and legislators in choosing between conflicting social and political theories. By then it will be clear that the kinds of theoretical issues raised by Lindblom and Habermas cannot be avoided. Indeed, we shall see that the prevailing approach to policy analysis is itself premised on a particular conception of politics, political practicality, and public problems. It could not be otherwise, for methodological principles about what phenomena to investigate, how to design research, and who to address with the findings, necessarily rest on substantive assumptions.

Chapter 2
Promise and Performance of the Great Society

CONCEPTUALLY and politically, it is impossible to disprove the premises of the Great Society. Conceptually, philosophers of science have shown that theoretical statements are immune to disconfirming evidence because the evidence can always be explained away by one or more "auxiliary hypotheses." When, for example, a planet fails to move in the path predicted by Newton's theory of gravity, analysts might hypothesize that some other planet is sufficiently near it to disturb its orbit. Much of science is concerned with investigating such claims. (For a discussion of auxiliary hypotheses, see Lakatos, 1970.)

The problem of auxiliary hypotheses is particularly troublesome in the analysis of public policy because demonstrations of policy failure can be challenged from two directions simultaneously. First, of course, is the issue of whether sufficient resources have been committed to a policy to allow its underlying assumptions to be tested. No president or political party ever gets everything requested, and hence, when policies fail, it is always possible to claim that more money or time or coordination was needed. Second, what counts as a fair test of a policy's success or failure is also debatable, particularly in light of inevitable questions about the adequacy of the resources committed to it. In most cases it is unreasonable to expect public policy to eliminate entirely a particular public problem, but incomplete results raise the issue of just how far a policy must go, and in exactly what direction, before it is judged "successful." With both of these lines of defense always available, it is impossible for program performance data to show conclusively that a given policy is misguided.

In the case of the Great Society the problem of auxiliary hypotheses centers around policy makers' notion of a "poverty culture."

17

The purpose of the Great Society was to eliminate poverty, not through a Robin Hood policy of taking from the rich and giving to the poor, but by bringing the poor into the mainstream of work, politics, and education. This general strategy was clear enough, as were policy makers' ideas about the specific programs needed to implement it, but a central question was left open: How much time, money, and effort would be needed before the poor were ready for full participation in the larger society?

The Great Society's Underlying Theories

Most explanations of poverty can be placed on a continuum that has as its basis the extent to which either the poor or the society is cited as the cause of poverty (Rose, 1972; Gordon, 1972; Levin, 1977). At one end of this continuum, poverty is attributed to inherent defects of the poor—their lack of ability, initiative, or persistence—and poverty is viewed either as an insolvable problem or as requiring for its solution changes in the poor. At the other end of the continuum, poverty is traced to characteristics of social, political, or economic organization, such as the drive of corporations for maximum profits or elite control over political resources. From this perspective, elimination or reduction of poverty would require changes in political, economic, or cultural institutions.

The Cycle of Poverty

The explanation of poverty that guided policy development under the Great Society falls close to the midpoint of this continuum. Policy makers did not see any fundamental defects in either the poor or the established institutions; they traced poverty to the separation of the poor *from* the institutions (Levine, 1970; Moynihan, 1968; Friedman, 1977; Aaron, 1978). The hypothesis was that the able-bodied poor are poor primarily because they are uneducated and indolent, but they have these poverty-generating characteristics because they live "in a world apart . . . isolated from the mainstream of American life and alienated from its values" (*ERP, historical and discipline - specific perspectives + theoretical 19 frameworks)*

1964, p. 55). The only institutionalized source of poverty identified was racial discrimination, which was viewed as a cultural phenomenon stemming from historical accident, not a natural product of private enterprise markets or other aspects of the political economy.

The basis for this explanation of poverty was a theory, developed implicitly in the policy process, that blended ideas prevalent during the 1950s in economics, political science, and sociology (Aaron, 1978).[1] Sociology provided the view that many of the poverty-causing characteristics of the poor stem from economic and political isolation. The theory was that unified configurations of norms and values—"subcultures"—are developed in response to environmental factors such as work options and systems of power. From this perspective, the poor develop deviant norms—a "culture of poverty" characterized by a short time horizon and limited ability to defer gratification—because they lack normal pathways for achievement. Drawing on the sociological theory that culture changes more slowly than social structure (a theory summed up by the concept of "cultural lag"), these norms were hypothesized to be highly resistant to change (Lewis, 1968; Moynihan, 1968).

The disciplines of economics and political science provided the argument that lack of opportunity is due to characteristics of the poor rather than to some defect in the political and economic systems. In political science, the group theory of politics dominant at the time suggested that the political system responds to organized interests and produces decisions reflecting a balance between the interests that are represented. By implication, the poor were hypothesized to lack access to the political system because they are not organized (Lowi, 1969; Rose 1972). In economics the Keynesian theory that unemployment stems primarily from inadequate demand was being challenged by the thesis that much unemployment is "structural," that is, due to a mismatch between labor force qualifications and independently evolving employment opportunities. In this view it was concluded that the poor lack employment opportunities because they lack appropriate skills and work motives (Kershaw and Levine, 1966; Lampman, 1965).

Together these theories suggested that poverty is self-perpetuating. In the conception of society underlying the Great Society (fig. 2-1), the cultural system is viewed as being composed of self-interested individuals whose motives and norms depend partly on their opportunities and partly on the culture transmitted to them by their parents and peers. The poor have developed a culture of poverty because they lack opportunity in the economic system and access to the political system. The political and economic systems do not provide them with access and opportunity because these systems, the theory suggests, accept only certain types of inputs. The political system responds primarily to organized interests, while the economic system accepts only skilled or at least properly socialized labor. Thus, there is a "cycle of poverty": Because the poor lack access to the political system and opportunity in the economic system, they develop antiwork norms and political cynicism, which in turn exclude them from the economy and polity.

The Policy Framework

The Great Society was launched with the Economic Opportunity Act (EOA) and the Civil Rights Act, both of which were passed in 1964 shortly after the assassination of President Kennedy. (For an overview of the programs comprising the Great Society and how they evolved, see Levitan, 1973; Levitan and Taggart, 1976; Friedman, 1977; Haveman, 1977.) The Economic Opportunity Act was funded initially at less than $1 billion, a paltry sum by later standards. The Civil Rights Act outlawed discrimination in employment and public accommodations, but it did not apply to sex discrimination and it included no requirements for affirmative action. Within a few years, though, these programs and laws mushroomed. By 1974, just a decade after the Great Society began, annual expenditures for social welfare totaled almost $140 billion (Skolnick and Dales, 1975, pp. 7–11). All told, between 1965 and 1980 the federal government spent $3.4 *trillion* on income and in-kind transfers and social programs.[2]

The Great Society had three basic components, which were designed to work together to break the cycle of poverty: (1) The

Figure 2-1. Conception of Society Underlying the Great Society

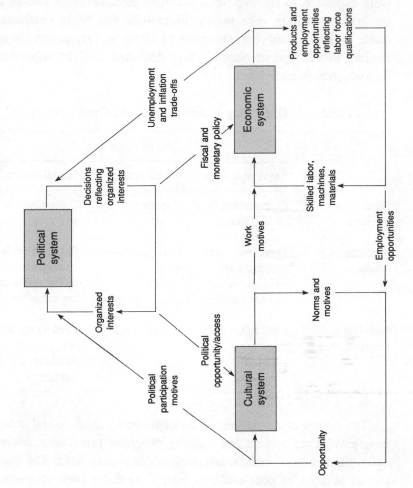

poor were socialized and educated so that they could gain entrance
to work, politics, and education; (2) unfair barriers to the economy,
polity, and culture were attacked; and (3) the resources of the poor
were expanded to remove the immediate environmental causes of
the poverty culture. The policy framework can be reconstructed
(table 2-1) by classifying a number of Great Society programs according to the type of benefits they delivered and the subsystem
into which they intervened.

Table 2-1. The Policy Framework of the Great Society

	Domain of intervention		
	Economic system	Political system	Cultural system
Social action programs	Occupational skills training	Community action	Compensatory education
Resource programs	Economic development; business assistance; income transfers [welfare]	Legal services	Community development; education and housing subsidies
Civil rights programs	Civil rights in employment	Voting rights	Civil rights in housing and public accommodations

The poor were socialized with what were called "social action
programs." Employment and training programs provided economically disadvantaged individuals with occupational skills. The intellectual abilities of poor children were remediated with compensatory education programs. And political organization of the poor was
stimulated by the Great Society's strategy for implementing antipoverty programs, a strategy that authorized community groups rep-
resenting the poor (Community Action Agencies) to participate in
both program planning and delivery.[3]
Prejudice and discrimination in political, economic, and cultural

institutions were attacked with civil rights legislation. The Voting Rights Act of 1965 was designed to dismantle racial barriers in the electoral system, and the Civil Rights Act of 1964 promoted equal access to housing, public accommodations, and employment. In the latter, discrimination on the basis of race, creed, color, or national origin was prohibited in hiring, discharge, promotion, transfer, training, and compensation, and in the sale, rental, and financing of most housing (Wallace, 1974).

The political, economic, and cultural resources made available to the poor included income, legal aid, medical care, small business development assistance and venture capital, loans and grants for higher education, and a variety of community development and housing subsidies.

These resources were delivered not simply or even primarily to ameliorate deprivation, but to alter the environment and expand the opportunities of the poor so as to break up the culture of poverty.[4] The delivery of resources through Community Action Agencies was designed in part to assure that resources were coordinated and concentrated on individual communities rather than spread thinly throughout a large geographical area.

In summary, the Great Society was built around the assumption that the characteristics of the poor, which supposedly maintain poverty, are highly resistant to change and are due to isolation from mainstream institutions. This assumption was not a minor underpinning; it was inherent in the design of the policy framework. In-kind transfers were used more heavily than cash to ameliorate economic deprivation because it was concluded, on the basis of the culture of poverty theory, that cash would simply have been absorbed into the poor's pathological life-style. Similarly, social action programs were designed to break up the hypothesized poverty culture, often by focusing on the young (who were thought to be more plastic than adults) and by taking program participants out of their regular environment (which was believed to be an active agent of malsocialization). In short, the Great Society was not supposed to be a welfare program.[5]

Effects of the Great Society

The effects of the Great Society have been identified in two basic ways. One method has been to take periodic measures of changes in the distribution and level of poverty on the assumption that the level of poverty should decline and the distribution should shift away from blacks as resource and social action programs break up the culture of poverty and as civil rights laws reduce discrimination. The other approach has been to assess the effects of individual antipoverty programs.

Changes in Poverty

Measuring Poverty. The U.S. government measures poverty with an income threshold, a level of income below which individuals are thought to be unable to meet their basic needs for food, shelter, and clothing. (For a summary of the history of this measure, see Rodgers, 1982, pp. 15–27.) The threshold was established by calculating the cost of a bare bones diet, the so-called economy diet developed by the Department of Agriculture. If it takes more than one-third of an individual's or family's income to purchase the food listed in the economy diet, then the individual or family is classified as poor. Income is counted before taxes and after any income transfers (such as Social Security benefits or welfare).[6]

This measure of poverty has been criticized for both underestimating and overestimating the amount of poverty. (For arguments that the measure underestimates the amount of poverty, see Rodgers, 1982, pp. 14–49; for arguments that it overestimates the amount of poverty, see Smeeding, 1975.) It underestimates poverty because it fails to indicate how poor the poor are relative to the poverty threshold and to the rest of the population. The amount of poverty in America as measured by the government would remain stable even if the poor fell further below the threshold or the poor became poorer in comparison to the general population. The government measure indicates how many people have incomes that fall below a certain point, not how far they fall or how high everyone else's income rises.

At the same time, the official measure of poverty *over*estimates poverty because it does not count people's assets or any government services they might receive, both of which may have substantial value. The assumption behind the measure is that most individuals need two-thirds of their income for housing, transportation, clothing, medical care, and other necessities in addition to food. However, if an individual owns outright a home and a car, then a very low income may be sufficient to meet his needs. Similarly, those who are eligible for one social program usually partake of several, and hence while their incomes may be low, their actual expenses may not be as great as the official measure of poverty assumes.[7] In short, the government measures income and ignores other sources of support.

Although the official measure of poverty is thus somewhat flawed, it is nevertheless consistent with the theory underlying the Great Society. If poor people are concentrated in urban ghettos and rural backwaters, and if most of them are unemployed and unemployable, then it makes sense to develop a measure to differentiate them from the rest of the population. Poor people are, in theory, an isolated, intractable mass.

How far a particular individual's income falls below the threshold, how many social services the individual receives from the government, or how far his income falls below the nation's median income is largely irrelevant. If poverty is a static condition, then a measure that draws a line between the poor and the nonpoor is quite appropriate.

Poverty Trends. Using this or similar measures, studies of the level and distribution of poverty have contributed a good deal of confusion to the debate over the Great Society because they have often focused on a very short period of time. Between 1965 and 1968, the percentage of all families in poverty declined from 13.9 to 10.0, roughly the level at which it remained throughout the 1970s.[8] On the face of it, this rapid reduction in the level of poverty and the ability to sustain the reduced level suggest that the Great Society was quite successful.

A major problem with this conclusion, however, is that it fails to take into account previous trends. Although the decline in poverty between 1965 and 1980 was substantial, much, if not all, of it would have occurred in the absence of antipoverty programs if poverty had simply continued to decline at previously established rates (fig. 2-2). If poverty had continued to decline at either the 1947–56 rate or the slower 1957–63 rate, by 1980 the percentage of families in poverty would have been between 10 and 13 solely as a result of general economic progress. In actuality, between 1965 and 1968 poverty declined much faster than in previous periods, but it then leveled off so that by 1980 there was little difference between projected and actual rates of poverty. In this sense, even with its expenditures for income transfers, the Great Society appears to have had no impact on the incidence of poverty among the general population.

A similar trend analysis shows that the Great Society's impact on the composition of the poverty population was to reduce the incidence of poverty among senior citizens and blacks (table 2-2, page 28). In the period 1947–62, only white families and families headed by males experienced above-average declines in poverty. In contrast, during the Great Society the rate of decline for white families slowed to the rate for all families, while the rates of decline for black families and senior citizens rose to considerably *above* average. The greater-than-average reduction of poverty among blacks in the 1966–80 period held for both male- and female-headed families.

In summary, then, the aggregate impacts of the Great Society were mixed. Although it was designed to help the poor earn their way out of poverty, the Great Society did not produce a reduction in poverty that exceeded what would have been expected to occur given pre-existing trends. The framework's only success appears to have been in diverting ongoing declines in poverty toward senior citizens and blacks. Since there was no net reduction in the incidence of poverty for the general population, this means that the Great Society's impact was a redistribution of poverty from blacks to whites, and from the old to the young.

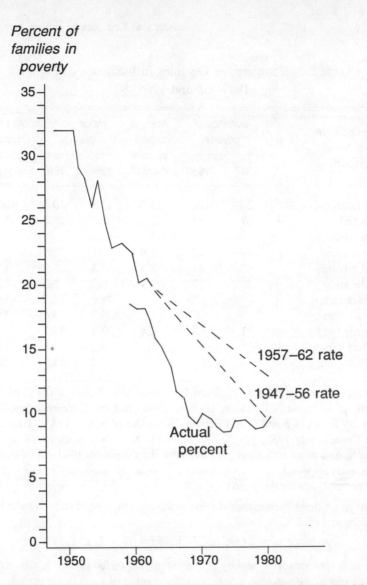

Percent of families in poverty

Figure 2-2. Trend Analysis of Families in Poverty, 1947–80

Sources: 1947–62 rates and 1980 projections are from the 1964 *Economic Report of the President,* pp. 59–60. 1959–80 rates are from "Money Income and Poverty Status of Families and Persons in the United States: 1981," Bureau of the Census, July 1982, p. 22, table 15.

Table 2-2. Comparative Declines in Incidence of Poverty,
1947–62 and 1966–80

Selected characteristics of household	Incidence of poverty		Average annual percent change[a]	Incidence of poverty		Average annual percent change[a]
	1947	1962		1966	1980	
All families	32	20	−2.5	11.8	10.3	−0.9
Head 65 and over	57	47	−1.2	28.5	15.7	−3.2
White family	29	17	−2.8	9.3	8.0	−0.9
Black family	67	44	−2.3	35.5	28.9	−1.3
Male head	30	17	−2.9	9.3	6.3	−2.3
Black family				27.6	14.3	−3.4
White family				7.7	5.6	−2.0
Female head	51	48	−0.4	33.1	32.7	−0.1
Black family				59.2	49.4	−1.2
White family				25.7	25.7	0.0

Sources: Rates for 1947 to 1962 are from *Economic Report of the President, 1964,* p. 71, table 7. Rates for 1966 to 1980 are from "Money Income and Poverty Status of Families and Persons in the United States: 1981," Bureau of the Census, July 1982, pp. 22–24, table 15. Note that incidence-of-poverty data broken down by race are not available for the period 1960–65. Likewise, incidence-of-poverty data broken down by head of household's race and sex are not available for the period 1947–62.

a. Average annual percentage change in the incidence of poverty is calculated as follows:

$$\text{Average annual percentage change} = [(I_1 - I_2) / I_1] / Y,$$

where I_1 = incidence of poverty in the initial year of the period, I_2 = incidence of poverty in the concluding year, and Y = number of years in the period.

Program Impacts

The Great Society's effects on the level and distribution of poverty can be traced to the impacts of individual programs comprising the policy framework. Overall, civil rights laws were relatively successful in achieving their intended objectives, but social action programs were not. Given that the former successfully manipulated the distribution of poverty across races, it makes sense that the framework's overall effect was a redistribution of poverty.

Social Action. The principal performance problem of social action programs was not so much their inability to produce expected impacts but the short life of the impacts that were achieved. Although some education programs were able to produce increases in the learning achievements and measured intelligence of disadvantaged children, these improvements were not maintained through the early elementary school years (Cicirelli et al., 1969). Moreover, when programs were developed to provide compensatory education through the public schools—in an attempt to maintain gains through the elementary school years—even the most promising of these programs also proved ineffective (Levin, 1977). The only effect compensatory education appears to have had is on the life choices of program participants, particularly regarding education. Participants were more likely than nonparticipants with similar backgrounds to complete high school and enter college, and less likely to be arrested or to have other problems (Berrueta-Clement, 1984).

Similar results were obtained from employment and training programs (Levin, 1977). Several programs out of the many that were tried produced gains in the earnings and employment of program participants. However, the gains were so modest that often they did not outweigh program expenditures, and in many instances where gains were observed, improvements in the earnings and employment of treatment groups relative to controls disappeared within eighteen months (Westat, Inc., 1978). The one target group that appeared to receive permanent benefits from employment and training programs was composed of new entrants into the labor market (Westat, Inc., 1978; Congressional Budget Office, 1982).

Finally, the evolution of Community Action Agencies, which were designed as a vehicle for organizing the poor politically, evidenced a similar pattern of early programmatic success followed by a decay in the gains achieved. Initially, many CAAs were quite radical and agitated for changes in the distribution of local government services. However, following the Model Cities Program, which gave elected officials control over program funding, most CAAs evolved into service agencies that had little if any effect on local government operations outside the antipoverty policy area (Rose, 1972; Peterson and Greenstone, 1977).

Income and In-Kind Transfers. The impacts and performance of in-kind and income transfer programs are difficult to assess because of the great variety of programs and the way they were studied. Significantly, transfer programs were never evaluated in terms of their combined effects on the hypothesized "culture of poverty." These programs have therefore proved to be the most controversial component of the Great Society. Defenders of the policy framework argue that transfer programs greatly improved the circumstances of the poor; critics claim that transfers undermined work motives and broke up families.

Considered individually, the programs that stand out as being visibly effective in mitigating deprivation include income transfers and medical aid. About half of the reduction in poverty following the Great Society was due to income transfers (Plotnick and Skidmore, 1975). Similarly, following the introduction of free medical care for the poor, the infant death rate dropped much more quickly than it had in preceding decades (Levitan and Taggart, 1976, p. 99). Also important were loans and grants for education, which led to rapid increases in college enrollment by the economically disadvantaged (Levitan and Taggart, 1976, pp. 129–30). Although at first additional education did not appear to lead to increased earnings (Levin, 1977; Jencks, 1972), by the mid-1970s educational investments by nonwhites began to pay off in higher incomes (Aaron, 1978, p. 93).

The evidence that transfers reduce labor force entry and break up families comes largely from several controlled experiments with income guarantees. Participants in the experiments were provided cash allowances which declined as work income increased. Results from these experiments varied significantly depending on the city in which they were conducted, the duration of the guarantee, and the instructions that were given to the participants. Overall, how-

ever, the studies indicated that income transfers do indeed reduce
work effort and labor force entry and do stimulate family breakups
(Bishop, 1980; Moffit, 1981). The negative effects on participants'
propensity to work were greatest for wives and single males, and
the dissolution of marriages was more frequent among black families than among white.

Civil Rights. In contrast to the disappointing performance of social action programs and the mixed performance of transfer programs, civil rights programs produced visible, long-lasting reductions in racial barriers to work and politics. Unquestionably, one of
the most successful programs in the Great Society was the Voting
Rights Act of 1965. Between 1960 and 1970, the percentage of the
nonwhite voting age population in the South that was registered to
vote rose from 29 to 60, and the number of black representatives in
southern state legislatures increased dramatically (Rodgers and Bullock, 1972). Likewise, affirmative action requirements under the
Civil Rights Act expanded employment opportunities for blacks,
and the earnings gap between blacks and whites diminished greatly,
becoming by the early 1970s almost zero for college graduates
(Levitan and Taggart, 1976, p. 131). The only area where civil
rights laws produced few if any visible results was in the sale of
private housing, an area where government enforcement abilities
are weak (Wallace, 1977).

Arguments in Defense of the Great Society

Clearly, the Great Society did not achieve its objective of
helping the poor earn their way out of poverty. The reductions in
poverty between 1965 and 1980 did not exceed what would have
been expected given pre-existing trends, and in any event they were
due mainly to income transfers rather than to enhanced earnings. To
be sure, the policy framework promoted political and economic
equality across races, and it helped the poor meet their needs for
food, housing, medical care, and other necessities. But it did not
succeed in moving the poor into the economic mainstream.

Despite this disappointing performance, defenders of the policy framework have offered two arguments for concluding that the thrust of the Great Society was basically sound. One argument is that there never really was a concerted attack on poverty. This claim has been made in both a moderate and an extreme form.

The extreme version asserts that the Great Society was really a myth. This is Michael Harrington's conclusion in *The New American Poverty* (1984, p. 15):

> There never really was a gigantic program of handouts to the poor, and to the minority poor in particular. . . . There never was a massive investment of billions of dollars in radical innovations that challenged the very structure of power in the United States. The spending was exceedingly modest, the programs largely unthreatening.

In part, Harrington's derision of the Great Society springs from his own radicalism, which leads him to contrast the antipoverty policy of the 1960s and '70s with the more fundamental changes he would like to have seen in the political and economic order. But Harrington's thesis is echoed by journalists and political pundits who claim that the Great Society was abandoned because of Vietnam. Many people believe that the Great Society was a short-lived burst of political rhetoric, not a genuine and sustained effort to eliminate poverty in America.

A moderate version of this argument is that there was indeed an attack on poverty, but for a variety of reasons it was unable to overcome the poverty culture. A great many analysts have followed Pressman and Wildavsky (1973) in suggesting that most antipoverty programs were never carried out as intended. An entire subfield has emerged in political science to study the implementation problems of social action, and it has left many with the impression that the Great Society failed because of bureaucratic inertia and mismanagement. In a similar vein, other analysts have argued that antipoverty programs were underfunded. To begin with, they point out correctly that roughly half of the Great Society's income and in-kind transfers went to the nonpoor (Aaron, 1978). The middle class benefited from loans and grants for higher education, health insurance for senior citizens under Medicare, loan guarantees for housing, and many other programs where income restrictions, if they existed at all, were well above the poverty line. Moreover, the argument continues, even those programs that were concentrated on the poor did not always reach the persons most in need. Plotnick and Skidmore (1975) have shown that income transfers were extensive enough in 1972 to have eliminated poverty entirely, but that because of variations between states in eligibility criteria and benefit levels, some people were lifted significantly above the poverty level while others were helped only modestly. In short, even if the Great Society was more than just opportunistic political rhetoric, perhaps it failed not because it was fundamentally misguided but because it was mismanaged, underfunded, and inadequately focused.

A second argument in defense of the Great Society is that the policy framework was reasonably successful. The claim here is not that the poor can now earn their way out of poverty, but rather that the standards used to judge the Great Society should be reconsidered.

Again, there is both a moderate and an extreme version of this argument. The moderate version—that the Great Society succeeded in making the nation a more just and equitable society—can be seen in the assessment by Sar Levitan and Robert Taggart (1976, p. 8):

> The results of government intervention varied, undesirable spillover effects occurred, and the adopted intervention strategies were sometimes ill designed; but progress was almost always made in the desired directions. The gains of blacks and the poor, the two primary target groups of federal efforts, offer the most striking evidence. Government programs significantly reduced poverty and alleviated its deprivations. Blacks made very significant strides in education, employment, income, and rights in the 1960s.

Levitan and Taggart are downplaying, if not ignoring, the claims

made by the policy makers who designed the Great Society. They
argue that the important point is not whether the policy framework
eliminated poverty and racial inequality but whether it moved society in that direction. Measured against this more modest standard,
the Great Society appears to have produced desirable results.

The more extreme argument is that the Great Society has actually gone quite far toward eliminating poverty altogether. This is
Schwarz's claim in *America's Hidden Success* (p. 32): "Perhaps the
best overall indicator of the substantial progress made by the nation
in the battle against poverty after 1960 is that by the second half of
the 1970s only 4 to 8 percent of the American public remained beneath the poverty level compared with about 18 percent in 1960."
The 4 to 8 percent figure cited by Schwarz is drawn from a number
of studies that calculated a dollar value for in-kind benefits and then
added the value to recipients' incomes before determining whether
individuals were above or below the poverty threshold (see Smeeding, 1975). Thus the conclusion that poverty has been drastically reduced ignores the Great Society's original objective of reducing
poverty by enhancing the earning power of the poor. Schwarz is
willing to abandon this goal because, as we saw in the preceding
chapter, he believes that certain groups will never be able to do well
in the private economy. If true, then the Great Society has done as
well as can be reasonably expected in eliminating poverty.

In short, when the results of the Great Society are examined
with the aim of assessing the policy framework's underlying assumptions, it appears that the policy framework may well have been
on the mark. Certainly, there is no conclusive evidence that the antipoverty policies of the 1960s and '70s were fundamentally misguided. Perhaps all that was needed for full success was more focus,
more money, or more time.

Chapter 3
A Shift in the Context of Evaluation

GIVEN OUR INABILITY to show that the Great Society's premises were faulty, one might ask how it was possible for the electorate to turn against it. The answer provided by many scholars is that the shift in public philosophy from the Great Society to the Reagan Revolution was based on broad contextual factors rather than on detailed knowledge of the impacts of the Great Society's programs. In the consensus seems to be that public policy moves through cycles of activism and withdrawal as first liberal and then conservative ideas play themselves out (see Hirschman, 1982; Heclo, 1986; Sawhill, 1986; Schlesinger, 1986; Sowell, 1987).[1] In this view, the Great Society was abandoned not because it failed to improve the earning capacity of the poor but because it was popularly identified, rightly or wrongly, with rising unemployment, inflation, and government waste.

How this conclusion is evaluated depends greatly on one's assumptions. Many analysts seem to believe that a more deep-thinking and logical public would have been skeptical of the Reagan philosophy. They have suggested that the citizenry's emphasis on broad, society-wide conditions is indicative of a shallow and largely uninformed perspective.

My own view is that there are actually important conceptual reasons to emphasize economic trends and social conditions more than program performance when evaluating policy frameworks. As we shall see, even though the theories underlying the Great Society and the Reagan Revolution each offered accounts of poverty, they conceptualized this phenomenon so differently that it is difficult, if not impossible, to compare the evidence supporting them. (For a detailed discussion of the problems encountered in trying to compare theories, see Fayerabend, 1970.) Some facts support both theo-

35

ries, while other facts are specific to only one theory. In this situation, what leads an analyst to favor one theory against the other is not some crucial finding about program performance but the ability of each theory to account for significant changes in social and economic conditions.

The Reagan Revolution

The theories underlying the Reagan Revolution are best understood as a critique of the Great Society, for the Reagan philosophy was developed in the context of electoral competition, and much of its empirical content deals with Great Society impacts. President Reagan and his advisors criticized the social and economic policies of the 1960s and '70s on four related grounds.

First, they argued that rather than reducing and mitigating the nation's poverty, the Great Society actually perpetuated and exacerbated it. The basis for this criticism was the theory of "welfare dependency" developed by George Gilder (1981). Like the cultural theory of poverty, welfare dependency theory assumes that the poor have dysfunctional attitudes, but it attributes these attitudes to unearned income and in-kind transfers rather than to a lack of opportunity. By giving females an income that is greater than what males can earn in low-wage jobs, the theory says, these programs weaken the male role in poor families, cause families to break up, and generate a class of single, separated, and divorced males whose culture dominates the poverty population (Gilder, pp. 83–94, 169–82). From this perspective, the key to overcoming unemployment and poverty is to reduce the economic independence of poor females. Accordingly, the Reagan administration's cuts in social programs were tailored toward this end.[2]

President Reagan's second line of argument was against the personal and corporate taxes associated with the Great Society's expansion of social services and income transfers. This criticism was founded on the so-called supply-side theory of economics developed by Ture (1980) and Laffer and Seymor (1979). According to the theory, the slow economic growth of the 1970s was caused in part by tax policies that discouraged saving, investment, and labor force entry. The Reagan administration acted on this argument by introducing, in the Economic Recovery Tax Act of 1981, the largest tax cut in American history. Accelerated depreciation of business equipment was supposed to lead to investment in fixed capital. Cuts in personal income and capital gains taxes were intended to promote saving and labor force entry. (For an overview of the tax cuts and their rationale, see Sawhill, 1982.)

The Reagan administration's third line of attack was made 3 against the fiscal and monetary policies introduced in the mid-1960s to fine-tune aggregate consumer demand. This argument was drawn from "monetarism," a theory developed several decades ago by Friedman (1962). Supposedly, repeated use of fiscal and monetary policy to stimulate production in the 1960s and '70s left in each instance a residue of higher inflation and generated inflationary expectations, requiring in turn an episode of monetary and fiscal restraint, which created yet another recession and led to another period of stimulus. All the while, inflation and unemployment ratcheted upward. A stable monetary policy was advocated by President Reagan as a way to eliminate inflationary expectations and return the economy to noninflationary economic growth.

Finally, a fourth line of criticism was developed to explain why 4 the Great Society's programs continued to be favored by the electorate even though, supposedly, they produced obvious problems. The Reagan administration argued that the political process is "overly responsive to special interests" (ERP, 1982, p. 39). In seeking to maximize their own welfare, voters tend to favor policies that benefit special interests because the benefits from such policies are highly concentrated and therefore quite visible, whereas the costs are spread thinly throughout the electorate and hence are hard to see. Even though the result of such policies, when viewed collectively by an outside observer, may be a decline in economic efficiency, which hurts everyone, the policies will be favored by "a coalition of minorities" (ERP, 1982, p. 38). As we have seen (in chapter 1), the administration's strategy of linking program cuts to tax cuts was designed to convince people to give up their pet benefits.

Together, these four lines of criticism present a picture that departs sharply from the image underlying the Great Society. In the conception of society implicit in the Reagan Revolution (fig. 3-1), the main source of the nation's problems is traced to the political system, which, in theory, promotes a special interest mentality by doling out benefits, discourages investment and production by taxing incomes heavily, and undermines work motives by providing welfare to poor females. The economic system is assumed to operate efficiently and at full capacity so long as markets are not hindered, and the cultural system is expected to generate acceptable motives if hard work is rewarded and hardworking family men are allowed to be community role models.

Assessing the Evidence

The electorate's judgment notwithstanding, it is not at all clear that the Reagan administration's charges against the Great Society are valid. That the downward trend in the incidence of poverty ended a few years after the Great Society began could be interpreted in at least two ways. It might be, as the Reagan philosophy suggests, that the Great Society halted the normal poverty reductions associated with economic growth. Alternatively, it is also possible that in the early 1970s economic growth finally came up against the "hard core unemployed," and the Great Society was simply unable to overcome the cultural defects of this group. The gross statistical evidence is simply inconclusive.

Moreover, even when we examine areas where the Great Society and the Reagan Revolution seem to be in direct conflict, the available data cannot decide the debate. One of the central disagreements dividing proponents of the two frameworks is over what produces the hypothesized culture of the poverty population and what can be manipulated to change it. There are at least two related questions at issue: (1) Is the culture of the poor due to isolation from mainstream institutions or instead to a shattered family structure destabilized by welfare? (2) To what extent will the poor benefit from economic growth?

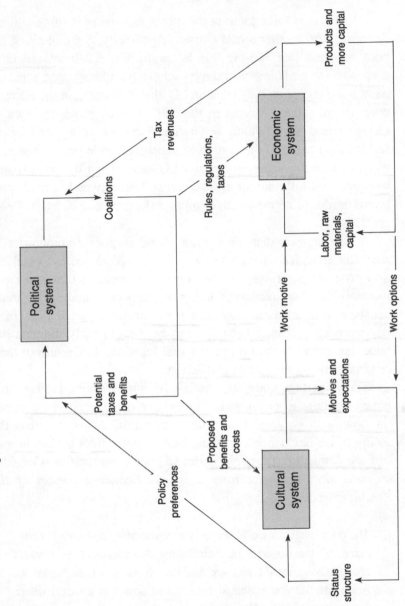

Figure 3-1. The Conception of Society Underlying the Reagan Revolution

The Culture of the Poor

There is little doubt at this point that the poor think and act differently from other social classes. Apparently, the culture of the poor is transmitted early in life. Economically disadvantaged children perform far below average on scholastic aptitude and achievement tests, and often they have an I.Q. that is lower than the norm in other income strata. Moreover, the culture is somewhat resistant to change. Head Start, which was targeted on the young and hence tackled the culture of the poor at its most malleable point, produced gains in learning achievement and I.Q. only when the participants were enrolled full time for at least a year. Half-day and summer programs produced no measurable impacts (Levitan and Taggart, 1976, pp. 124–25).

It also appears that the culture found in poor communities is powerful enough to overcome most changes produced by social action. The temporariness of the impact of social action programs indicates that there are forces acting on the poor to make them think and behave in a certain way. The poor can be removed from their environment, and their behavior can be demonstrably altered. But once they return to their original social location, they return to their original patterns of thought and action.

The important question, though, is what factors produce the poverty culture to begin with. The culture of poverty theory traces the culture to isolation from mainstream institutions, whereas the theory of welfare dependency says that it comes from broken homes and the dominance of single males in poor communities. Consider the following statement from the 1964 *Economic Report of the President* (p. 55):

> The poor inhabit a world scarcely recognizable, and rarely recognized, by the majority of their fellow Americans. It is a world apart, whose inhabitants are isolated from the mainstream of American life and alienated from its values. It is a world where Americans are literally concerned with day-to-day survival—a roof over their heads, where the next meal is coming from. It is a world where a minor illness is a major tragedy, where pride and

privacy must be sacrificed to get help, where honesty can become a luxury and ambition a myth. Worst of all, the poverty of the fathers is visited upon the children.

Now contrast the analysis above with the explanation provided by Gilder (1981, pp. 90–91):

> The key to lower-class life in contemporary America is that unrelated individuals, as the census calls them, are so numerous and conspicuous that they set the tone for the entire community. . . . The short-sighted outlook of poverty stems largely from the breakdown of family responsibilities among fathers. The lives of the poor, all too often, are governed by the rhythms of tension and release that characterize the sexual experience of young single men. . . . The key to the intractable poverty of the hardcore American poor is the dominance of single and separated men in poor communities. . . . The problem is neither race nor matriarchy in any meaningful sense. It is familial anarchy among the concentrated poor of the inner city, in which flamboyant and impulsive youths rather than responsible men provide the themes of aspiration.

The available evidence from research on the Great Society cannot tell us which, if either, of these explanations of the poverty culture is correct. Even if, as the Reagan administration claims, welfare is associated with divorce, this does not mean that divorce and the corresponding increase in single males necessarily creates a "welfare culture," a culture of "flamboyant and impulsive youths." Conversely, the observation by theorists for the Great Society that the poor tend to be isolated in "a world apart" need not imply that the poverty culture comes from isolation and deprivation.

Of course, it might be possible to design research to resolve this issue. In fact, this will be suggested in chapter 8. But even if such research were conducted, it would leave a number of questions unanswered, perhaps most important among them questions about the stability and foundations of the culture of the larger society. Al-

could be neither :

though we might be successful in identifying the sources of the pathological culture of poor communities, we would still not know how to deal with that culture unless we had similar knowledge about the motivations of the general population. If the mainstream culture is stable, then the poverty culture could be attacked without fear of disrupting important social processes. On the other hand, if the Reagan philosophy is correct that most people are concerned only about their immediate economic opportunities, then we might decide that the poverty culture is an unfortunate, but nevertheless unavoidable, condition of modern societies.

The Benefits of Economic Growth

Whether economic growth benefits the poor is also unclear. Setting aside for the moment the issue of what factors generate the peculiar attitudes and behaviors of poor people, the question boils down to whether the poor are capable of participating in the economy. The assumption of the Great Society was that the poor have weak work motives and limited skills and are trapped in jobs that provide low wages and only intermittent employment. The assumption of the Reagan Revolution is that the poor are capable of skilled labor or at least are capable of saving for training and getting the skills they need to get ahead. From this latter perspective, a rise in national income will benefit the poor if welfare cuts are successful in forcing them back into the labor force. The issue, then, is whether poverty is a room with no exit or, instead, the bottom rung of a ladder that the poor refuse to climb.

The best research available for addressing this issue is the Panel Study on Income Dynamics, which tracked a sample of five thousand families (both poor and nonpoor) over a six-year period (Lane and Morgan, 1975). The study found that, of those families in poverty at the beginning of the research in 1967, 39 percent were also in poverty when the research ended in 1972. On the other hand, over half of those who were poor at the start of the study were not poor at the end (that is, their family income exceeded the official poverty line), and, of the families that escaped poverty, over half ended up with incomes at least 50 percent above the official poverty line. These findings have led at least one analyst (Aaron, 1978) to conclude that poverty is often a very transitory state.[3] However, the Panel Study, questioning the arbitrarily defined poverty line, also showed that when an income 50 percent above the official poverty line is used as the poverty threshold, the poor are a fairly stable group over time (Lane and Morgan, 1975, p. 35).

Clearly, the findings from the Panel Study are equivocal. The problem is that the research focused on the poverty threshold and simply measured changes in status relative to it. The observation that there is a considerable amount of movement around the poverty line can be interpreted in two ways. If the poverty threshold is taken as a valid indicator of poverty, then the Great Society appears mistaken in its premise that the poor are stuck in an income trap. After all, over half of the people in poverty today will be out of poverty within six years. If, conversely, it is assumed that the poverty threshold is simply a rough indicator, then the income changes observed in the Panel Study seem modest at best. Most people who have low incomes today will have low incomes five years from now, even though some of them may experience slight increases.

Again, though, even if we could resolve this issue, we would still not know what to do about poverty. For one thing, it is not at all clear what governs the economic structure. Perhaps, as the Reagan Revolution assumes, it is technology and investment that need to be manipulated to promote economic growth and reduce deprivation, but it might also be property rights or the organization of labor or the form of the business enterprise. On this point, evidence from policy research is mute, and the Reagan Revolution is based largely on faith.

Moreover, knowledge of the key variables responsible for poverty would not necessarily dictate a particular policy. Even if it were concluded that poverty can be reduced only by somehow stimulating investment, many other factors would have to be considered. It might be, as the Reagan administration has argued, that an economic expansion coupled with reductions in welfare will generate initiative and hard work in the lower classes, but accompanying this might be a reduction in popular control of government, a shift in

public opinion toward intolerance, and widespread suffering from
business relocations and automation. Again, once the argument
moves from questions about poverty to larger issues about the social and economic structure, evidence on antipoverty programs has
little, if anything, to offer.

The Importance of Social Conditions

Evaluating public policy is not a straightforward matter of
weighing the evidence for and against various theories. The problem is that different theories will attach different weights to the
same evidence, key facts can be interpreted in various ways, and
certain findings will be important from one perspective but not another. Although it may be possible to develop crucial tests where
conflicting theories are pitted against each other in the same domain
of inquiry, the results from such tests do not speak for themselves,
and, in any event, they will inevitably fail to answer important
questions that lie beyond the scope of the research.   relevant

What seems to have convinced the electorate to abandon the
Great Society was not some narrow fact about program performance
or even the persistence of high levels of poverty in the 1970s; it was
a rapid rise in inflation and unemployment. Between 1948 and
1978, six recessions occurred, one each in 1948, 1954, 1957, 1960,
1969, and 1973 (fig. 3-2). Except for the expansions leading up to
the 1969 and 1973 recessions—expansions where unemployment
declined to 3.5 and 4.9 percent respectively—the unemployment
rate was successively higher during each expansion, beginning at a
low of 2.9 percent in 1953 and rising to 4.1 percent in 1956, 5.5
percent in 1960, and 5.8 percent in 1978. Concomitantly, the level
to which inflation had been declining during recessions rose
steadily from −0.4 percent in 1955, to 0.8 percent in 1959, 1 percent
in 1961, 3.3 percent in 1972, and 5.8 percent in 1976. By 1979
when the presidential election campaigns were under way, inflation
was running at double-digit levels while unemployment hovered
stubbornly above 5 percent. The Reagan argument was that this

"stagflation" was due to welfare, high taxes, and a stop-and-go monetary policy.

The thesis that Ronald Reagan's victory in 1980 marked a turn in electoral and ideological cycles is surely correct, but it says nothing about the substantive way in which this shift occurred. The emergence of stagflation led to a reinterpretation of evidence that earlier had seemed trivial. We can see this clearly by recalling how the impacts of the Great Society appeared in the previous chapter when we were working exclusively from premises of the cultural theory of poverty. The finding that welfare undermines work motives seemed unimportant. It was easily overshadowed by the desirable effects welfare had on infant mortality, hunger, and access to housing and education. So long as the poor are thought of as culturally defective and socially isolated, the most important issue is whether social programs are improving their circumstances, not what effects these programs are having on market efficiency, work motives, or marital stability. It is this conceptual blindness that must have been responsible for the nation's failure to question the Great Society in the early 1970s. Even though wage and price controls had been introduced because of inflation and policy makers were already aware that welfare undermines work motives, spending for social programs grew steadily.

However, once inflation and unemployment reached levels that gave real credence to the arguments of Friedman, Laffer, Gilder, and other conservative intellectuals, the nation's perception of the Great Society went through a gestalt shift. Welfare's undesirable effects on labor force entry were linked conceptually to the rapidly rising unemployment and inflation of the 1970s, and suddenly it was *these* impacts that were important, not the proven ability of social programs to mitigate deprivation. A single fact—stagflation —led to a change in theoretical orientation that altered the weights attached to all the other evidence.

It was not that the theories underlying the Great Society were incapable of providing an explanation of the stagflation phenomenon. As we have seen, the Great Society's designers attributed unemployment to a mismatch between available jobs and labor force

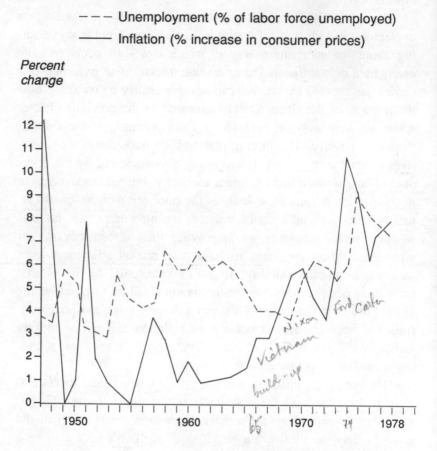

Figure 3-2. Unemployment and Inflation, United States, 1948–78.
Data from *Manpower Report of the President,* 1979.

qualifications. In their view, deficit spending and low interest rates would cause wage and price inflation if the unemployed were not employable; the pressure of consumer demand would lead employers to bid against each other for suitable employees. This line of reasoning was applied to explain the stagflation of the 1970s. At the time, many more women than normal were entering the labor market because of the women's movement, and the labor force was also becoming younger because the baby boom generation was reaching adulthood. Hence analysts argued that the "natural" rate of unemployment was rising because many women and young people were not yet ready for employment, and they said that subsequent efforts to reduce unemployment to the levels experienced in the 1960s, along with the oil embargo and rising energy costs, were causing inflation.

At some point this argument simply lost its persuasiveness. Perhaps it was because the upward trend in inflation and unemployment could be traced back to the 1950s, long before the labor market swelled with women and youths. Alternatively, people may have questioned the structural unemployment hypothesis once they saw that the massive job training and employment programs of the 1970s—programs that had been initiated in response to the claim that certain segments of the labor force needed skills and work experience—were associated with an increase in inflation and unemployment rather than a decline. Many other factors could have been responsible for the electorate's ideological shift.

The important observation is that the outcome of the theoretical conflict between the Great Society and the Reagan Revolution hinged on a broad social indicator, not on narrow facts about program performance. The Reagan philosophy made sense in 1980 because, at the time, inflation and unemployment were at alarming levels, and the problem of stagflation was central to the empirical content of supply-side economics and monetarism. In contrast, the cultural theory of poverty—a set of ideas developed mainly to explain "poverty amidst affluence"—while adaptable to the new situation, nevertheless seemed off target, particularly as unemployment and inflation rose while antipoverty programs were expanded.

Center vs Periphery:
world/systems theoretical sectoral analysis
needed: subsidies and internal colonization

It is worth noting that the Reagan Revolution will likewise probably stand or fall on the basis of broad social and economic conditions rather than on how it affects labor force entry, saving, investment, or its other immediate targets. Currently, the central issue is the budget deficit. There are sound theoretical reasons for the persistent budget shortfall to raise doubts about the Reagan program, notwithstanding the program's apparent success in "defeating" inflation. During the debates between the presidential candidates in 1980, Ronald Reagan said that taxes could be cut, defense spending could be expanded, and the federal budget could be balanced, all at the same time. The basis for this claim was the thesis from supply-side economics that tax cuts would be self-financing because they would lead workers in the underground economy to reenter the labor force and investors to shift from tax shelters to productive activities, thus broadening the tax base. That budget deficits rose to and remained at unprecedented levels throughout the 1980s casts serious doubts on supply-side premises. Whether the policy framework can withstand this anomaly remains to be seen; no doubt it will depend somewhat on economic trends. A spurt in inflation, a stock market crash, or a serious economic recession could be tied back to the deficit by the framework's critics and lead to yet another gestalt shift in public philosophy.

Implications for Policy Analysis

Our analysis up to this point has at least two implications for policy research. First, it shows the importance of using more than one theory in identifying impacts and interpreting findings. A multiple-theory approach acts as a sort of conceptual magnifying glass, allowing analysts to see aspects of public policy that are overlooked by those who simply adopt the viewpoint of policy makers. Indeed, insofar as analysis is restricted to a single theory or point of view, problems in program performance will not appear as problems at all. (This point has been made in the philosophy of science by Lakatos, 1970, in his criticisms of Kuhn.) Policy analysts need conflicting theories to be able to observe unintended impacts and place them in a context where their potential consequences can be seen.

The second implication is that policy analysis should have a broad scope. Policy analysts have been trying to achieve theoretical progress through precise measurement and a narrow focus, and yet this is like trying to look at an elephant through a microscope. The observations that really seem to matter in debates over policy frameworks involve society-wide or systemic conditions, not assessments of program performance. Hence policy analysts need to step back from the subject matter and concentrate on the relationship between public policy and the overall political-economic system, replacing their methodological microscope with a theoretical "macroscope."

Chapter 4
Lindblom's *Politics and Markets*

THE NARROW FOCUS of most program evaluations follows directly from a questionable, and yet largely unquestioned assumption of U.S. public policy. For at least the past thirty years, policy makers have assumed that people's beliefs, intentions, and aspirations are rooted in their immediate circumstances. The Great Society was premised on the belief that individuals who have a certain amount of economic security, and who are presented with a range of opportunities, develop a personal philosophy that is essentially democratic and oriented toward the public good. This belief was behind the Great Society's political strategy of appealing to the nation's conscience, which was assumed to be based solidly in middle- and upper-class social conditions, and it was also implicit in the policy of trying to eliminate the poverty culture by improving conditions and expanding employment opportunities in poor communities. Similarly, the Reagan Revolution assumed that people choose their goals and form their intentions on the basis of the social and economic trade-offs confronting them. The idea of trying to sell budget cuts by packaging them with tax cuts rested on the belief that most Americans assess policy in terms of how it affects them personally and in the short run; the strategy of cutting welfare to get poor females to treat their mates with respect presumed that a similar logic is operative in the day-to-day decisions of the lower class.

For mnemonic purposes we can refer to this assumption as the premise of situational determinism. The thesis that behavior is situationally determined justifies a narrowly focused approach to policy analysis because it implies, first, that the most important aspect of public policy is how it affects the proximate situation of a given

population, and, second, that the impacts of policy will be limited to
changes in the motivations of the population in question.

Lindblom offers us new insights into the Great Society precisely
because he rejects the thesis that motivation is an individualistic,
contextually dependent phenomenon. His view is that people's motives are formed on the basis of the options presented to them not
by their immediate circumstances but in the ideologies, appeals, arguments, and propaganda developed by elites in an ongoing competition of ideas.

In *Politics and Markets* he argues that the relationship between
government and the economy determines the nature of this ideological competition and thus influences the beliefs and intentions of
different subgroupings, including the poor. In the next chapter we
shall see that this set of premises shifts the focus of policy analysis
from questions about how the Great Society affected the poor to the
issue of how it altered political discourse and popular demands.
First, though, we must gain a detailed understanding of Lindblom's
theory.

Politico-Economic Mechanisms

Politics and Markets is Lindblom's response to an argument in political science over the relative merits of liberal democracy and socialism.[1] Critics of liberal democracies have argued that
capitalism is in conflict with accepted democratic values in at least
three respects. Large corporations, the critics claims, are able to
exert too much control over government because of their ability to
make large campaign contributions; furthermore, the private sector
operates as a kind of private government by virtue of the power of
corporations to make decisions that have public consequences for
which the corporations are not held publicly accountable; and, third,
the business enterprise is itself undemocratic in its internal authority relations (Miliband, 1969; Preston, 1984; Bowles and Gintis,
1986). Defenders of liberal democracy have argued back that
business interests are counterbalanced by such powerful groups as

organized labor and consumers; that if business is internally undemocratic, then so are schools, interest groups, and most other
organizations in modern society; and that, in any event, government
already regulates many business activities and additional regulation
risks damaging the economy and violating people's basic rights
(see Friedman, 1962; Nozick, 1974; Vogel, 1987; Berger, 1986).

Lindblom's earlier writings were clearly in the camp of the
liberal democrats (see, e.g., Dahl and Lindblom, 1953; Lindblom,
1959, 1965, 1968). In the 1950s and '60s he was a defender of pluralism—the theory that power in the liberal democracies is fragmented and balanced rather than concentrated in the hands of an
elite or ruling class—and he made a very cogent argument in favor
of an incremental approach to policy making. Both pluralism and
incrementalism were developed in defense of liberal democracy and
in opposition to calls for socialism. However, in *Politics and Markets* Lindblom shifts his position and argues that the choice between
liberal democracy and socialism is really a false dilemma (Lindblom, 1977, pp. 248–53). The concerns voiced by the advocates of
each type of political-economic system are legitimate, he says, but
it is possible to form a hybrid third type that combines the best
aspects of both systems.

Lindblom's starting point for this conclusion is the thesis that
social organization is governed by "politico-economic mechanisms." People can be controlled, he says, either by being told what
to do, by being persuaded to do it, or by being given something to
induce them to perform the desired action. From these three "methods of social control"—authority, exchange, and persuasion—the
world's political-economic systems have developed. Exchange relations are the basis of markets, authority is the foundation of government and other formal organizations, and persuasion underlies education, advertising, and political propaganda.

Lindblom argues that historically the main choice of politico-
economic mechanisms in national systems has been between authority and exchange, each of which performs some functions well
but others poorly. What distinguishes one system from another is
the extent to which markets displace government or government

displaces markets, a distinction that for Lindblom explains the kinds of politics associated with different systems. "In an untidy process called politics," he says, "people who want authority struggle to get it while others try to control those who hold it" (p. 119).[2] Although authority is constrained by rules, by the need for cooperation from government officials, and in some systems by procedures designed to achieve popular control over authority, authority is never completely controlled because "people with authority can always find some loophole to make possible its extended use," that is, its use for the purpose of increasing authority by creating "informal authority structures" (pp. 25, 129). Consequently, claims Lindblom, "politics, though varying from country to country, comes to be in large part not a pyramidal exercise of authority but a vast, complex set of mutual interactions" (p. 122).

The relationship between politics and markets is that markets create a set of business leaders who are to some extent independent of governmental leaders and who exercise a countervailing authority that limits the government's extension of its authority. In politico-economic systems that attempt to replace markets with government, such "rival controls" are eliminated, and the struggle for authority in such systems is less pluralistic, in the sense that fewer organizations are involved in the struggle. Thus the nature of politics, public discourse, and popular opinion is traced back to the particular kinds of controls exercised by government over the economy.

Because he analytically decomposes politico-economic systems into the politico-economic mechanisms of authority, exchange, and persuasion, Lindblom is able theoretically to recombine these mechanisms in new ways. In particular, Lindblom's analytic approach allows him to undermine the categorical choice between capitalism and socialism by suggesting that exchange in markets is independent of the distribution of property rights and the form of authority in business enterprises. For Lindblom, class inequalities are the result not of markets but of "a historical inequality in the distribution of wealth," where "owners of capital have become the owners of the enterprise" (p. 105). Viewing this inequality as a

"separable effect" of markets, Lindblom claims that market systems
are possible that eliminate inequality of income and wealth. From
this perspective, markets can be maintained so that liberty is protected by a division of authority between government and business
leaders, while at the same time equality can be achieved through redistributions of income and changes in corporate ownership. Thus,
whereas socialists have argued that equality requires the dissolution
of markets and liberal democrats have argued that liberty requires
the maintenance of privately owned corporations, Lindblom claims
that both liberty and equality can be promoted by a particular combination of exchange and authority. Lindblom sketches such a system after explaining the political disabilities of existing systems.

Existing Political-Economic Systems

Lindblom divides modern political-economic systems into
three basic categories, although his theory suggests there is a fourth,
as yet untried, possibility. For purposes of clarification, he offers (p.
161) the table here renumbered 4-1. The horizontal dimension
(polyarchic versus authoritarian) characterizes the political-eco-

Table 4-1. Political-Economic Systems

	Polyarchic	Authoritarian
Market-oriented systems (not exclusive of authority)	All polyarchal systems: North America, Western Europe, and others	Most of the world's systems, including Yugoslavia, Spain, Portugal, most of Latin America, new African nations, the Middle East except Israel, and all of noncommunist Asia except Japan
Centralized authority and preceptoral "systems" (not exclusive of market)		Communist systems except Yugoslavia and perhaps Hungary

nomic systems' governments, distinguishing between governments that do and do not have elections between competing elites, freedom of expression, freedom of association, and other formal rules and procedures ensuring that authority is kept within bounds. The vertical dimension (market-oriented systems versus centralized authority and preceptoral systems) characterizes the way political-economic systems organize production, dividing systems into those that use markets for making most decisions about what is produced and in what quantity, and those that attempt to coordinate production authoritatively. With his theory Lindblom is able to explain the type of politics associated with each of these existing systems.

Polyarchy

Polyarchy is Lindblom's name for liberal democracy. It is a political system designed to constrain authority so that certain liberties are protected, including private property, free enterprise, free contract, and occupational choice. Lindblom argues that all existing polyarchies have market-oriented economies not because of some intrinsic tie between polyarchies and markets, but because polyarchic authority systems and modern market systems have a common origin: Polyarchic authority was established to protect the liberties necessary for modern markets. Lindblom calls the type of market system historically associated with polyarchy a "private enterprise market system." In such a system, individuals who own or operate a business enterprise are free to make decisions about what to produce, who to hire and fire, when to invest, where to locate, and so on.

According to Lindblom, politics in market-oriented polyarchies suffers to some extent from what he calls "circularity," where citizens are persuaded through a "lopsided competition of ideas" to buy and to vote for what elites are already disposed to grant them (pp. 201–2). Stemming from the privileged position of business in government and from the discretion available to business leaders in the operation of business enterprises, this circularity is evidenced in both political and economic choice, and it is reinforced by the effects of social class. In economic choice, there is competition be-

tween products, but informed choice is undermined because consumers are persuaded by advertising that "buying is the way to pop-
ularity, honor, distinction, delight and security" (p. 216). In politics
businessmen gain influence disproportionate to their numbers because they control crucial resources and participate more frequently
than other persons. As a result, the "business message" dominates
public debate and citizens are conditioned to accept uncritically the
authority that businessmen have. Reinforcing this conditioning,
says Lindblom, are powerful incentives for lower socioeconomic
classes to conform to the characteristics of the "favored class,"
adopting the favored class's belief in "private enterprise, private
property, corporate autonomy, and opportunities for great wealth"
(p. 226).

The most important consequence of this conditioning is to remove "primary issues" from politics, that is, issues concerning
private enterprise, corporate autonomy, income distribution, and the
relationships between business and government and business and
labor. Hence, says Lindblom, the struggle for authority in these systems tends to center around a narrow range of "secondary issues,"
and citizens' volitions are "constrained." Lindblom summarizes this
conclusion as follows (pp. 211–12).

> On how these constraints are achieved, the analysis traces them
> back to the duality of leadership in these systems, to the
> consequent privileged position of business, and to the dispropor-
> tionate influence of business in polyarchy. . . . The constraints
> are not consistent with the democratic theory or ideology often
> invoked to justify these systems. In the polyarchies, core beliefs
> are the product of a rigged, lopsided competition of ideas.

Communist Systems

In contrast to the duality of leadership in market-oriented
polyarchies, communist systems are characterized by Lindblom as
having a great concentration of political authority (p. 238). Although these systems have a "polyarchal facade," their authority is

less constrained by rules and by constitutionalism than is authority in market-oriented polyarchies. Top leadership employs a privileged, mobilizing organization—the political party—that controls the government and indoctrinates the citizenry with an official ideology.

In communist systems, the government owns most productive assets and immediately and directly organizes the economy. Although consumer and labor markets are allowed to operate, intermediate markets are disestablished, and the government in effect allocates inputs to business enterprises by setting prices and quotas for the production of all goods. In the place of market incentives to motivate productivity and innovation, communist systems use moral incentives and political indoctrination, but owing to the stifling influence of bureaucracy these incentives cannot stimulate production to the level attained by private enterprise market systems.

Whereas market-oriented polyarchies are characterized by Lindblom as having a certain amount of circularity in their politics and markets, communist systems evidence for Lindblom such an extreme degree of circularity that he calls them "preceptoral systems." A preceptoral system is "a system of social control through highly unilateral governmental persuasion addressed not to an elite or to a bureaucracy alone but to an entire population" (p. 54). While politics in communist systems has a certain amount of pluralism, in the sense that the bureaucracy, the military, and the political party compete for control of the government, the principle of pluralism is repressed, and citizens are denied freedom of thought, speech, religion, assembly, and movement, as well as privacy. With unchecked authority, top leaders use the political party to indoctrinate citizens so that they pursue collective goals "voluntarily." Thus, although for Lindblom communist systems are much more egalitarian than market-oriented polyarchies, they have much less liberty.

Market-Oriented Authoritarian Systems

Lindblom has relatively little to say about what can be called "market-oriented authoritarian systems," but he does devote a chapter to Yugoslavia, which is in this category. Yugoslavia is especially interesting to him because it recently shifted from a command economy to a form of "market socialism," where publicly owned and worker-controlled business enterprises make production decisions on the basis of profitability rather on the basis of quotas established centrally. For Lindblom, the fact that in Yugoslavia markets have been combined with new forms of authority in the business enterprise supports his contention that markets are independent of private enterprise.

Although Yugoslavia has the authoritarian government characteristic of communist systems, it has been moving away from a command economy since 1952. In 1965 it implemented major reforms reducing central administrative control over production to interventions through taxation, subsidies, and industry-specific regulations—much like the administrative controls in market-oriented polyarchies. However, unlike the private enterprise market system associated with polyarchy, the market system in Yugoslavia is composed of publicly owned enterprises that are run at least in part by trade unions and workers' councils. Nevertheless, the Yugoslavian business enterprise purchases labor in labor markets and materials in intermediate markets, it sells its products in consumer markets, and it is free to seek new markets, to diversify its production, and to divide its profits among wages, worker benefits, and reinvestment.

The long-term effects on Yugoslavian politics of the transition to a market economy are, Lindblom says, uncertain, but some effects are predictable and explicable from Lindblom's theory. Unavoidably, claims Lindblom, a market-oriented economy requires that the business enterprise be given sufficient authority to make decisions on the basis of market conditions, and this, he says, will lead to a division of leadership between business and government (or party) and to a "privileged position" for enterprise management. Moreover, given the form of authority within the Yugoslavian business enterprise, i.e., worker control, "it is possible that the prerogatives of businessmen in the private enterprise systems will become the prerogatives of groups of employees in each firm [in Yugoslavia's market socialism]" (p. 342). If so, Yugoslavian politics would undoubtedly become more pluralistic, but it would suffer from having economic control divided up into "islands of monopoly."

In summary, then, Lindblom argues that the combination of politico-economic mechanisms in each category of existing political-economic systems has certain inadequacies. Legitimated by a theory that offers more than human beings can deliver, communist systems attempt to coordinate production authoritatively. As a result, not only are they inefficient in economic choice, they also leave government and party leaders unchecked by any countervailing authority, and government leaders are able to indoctrinate citizens through the unilateral persuasion of a preceptoral system. Likewise, although the market socialism of Yugoslavia is in theory likely to lead to relatively pluralistic politics, Lindblom suggests that this pluralism by itself will be problematic, since even worker-controlled business enterprises are likely to develop privileges similar to those of business enterprises in the polyarchies. Finally, existing polyarchies evidence circularity in political and economic choice because business leaders in these systems condition citizens not to question their authority. Implicit in Lindblom's critique of existing political-economic systems is an ideal system.

Lindblom's Ideal

For Lindblom, liberty requires that citizens be free to choose from an unconstrained set of competing ideas. In evaluating existing political-economic systems, Lindblom finds such liberty thwarted even in polyarchies, which claim to value it, and he explains this phenomenon by arguing that the privileged position of business in private enterprise market systems leads to imbalances in the competition between organizations and their corresponding ideas. Consistent with this explanation, Lindblom suggests that both liberty and equality would be increased if existing polyarchies were restructured so that corporate discretion is brought under popular control. Throughout *Politics and Markets,* but particularly at the end of the book, Lindblom argues that the best practical way to accomplish this would be with "a hybrid form of popular control" that combines market control over production with the controls of a more "collectivist" polyarchy over the corporate decisions on which market control is weak (pp. 156–57, 349). Specifically, Lindblom prescribes modifications designed to correct the problems he identified in his analysis of existing polyarchies: fragmented authority in government, and the unregulated discretion of corporations.

In order to overcome the privileged position of business in market-oriented polyarchies, Lindblom advocates extending government control over business decisions. The most specific suggestion he makes along these lines is what he calls a "planner sovereignty market system." "In the fullest form of planner sovereignty," he says, "all production, consumer goods included, would be guided by the purchases of a government that has displaced the consumer as the 'sovereign'."[3] As Lindblom notes, all market-oriented systems are in part planner sovereignty systems because their governments buy many final products, particularly military weapons, highways, medical services, and education. By extending this planner sovereignty over more products, Lindblom suggests, governments could coordinate productive activities without using price controls and assigned targets and quotas. With planner sovereignty markets, the government could manipulate consumption patterns by raising the prices for some products and lowering them for others, and it could also control business enterprises by, Lindblom says, paying businesses to waive some of their privileges.

Although Lindblom believes a move to worker or publicly controlled corporations would promote liberty and equality more than does private enterprise, he defends a retention of private enterprise under planner sovereignty on the grounds that more blatant actions might "awaken" business.[4] The purpose of a planner sovereignty market system is to subject business enterprises to polyarchic authority without destroying the market's ability to coordinate production and promote innovation and diversity of opinion. The practical problem in implementing such controls is that business leaders consistently resist any intrusions by government into their activities, claiming, from Lindblom's perspective incorrectly, that such intrusions undermine both market efficiency and democracy. However, in the aerospace and defense industries, corporations have been willing to tolerate a great deal of regulation in return for financial indulgence, and Lindblom argues that other industries may be willing to do the same if planner sovereignty is extended further. Admittedly, Lindblom says, this approach does not guarantee success, "for it may be that at some point it awakens business leadership, passive as it appears to be in the defense industries, to a new and universal threat to its influence in the nation and world" (p. 351). But, Lindblom argues, "the strategy points to a road down which policy could possibly travel for some great distance" (p. 351).

In order to correct the "disabilities of mutual adjustment" in existing polyarchies, that is, the way in which authority is excessively fragmented, Lindblom proposes "a less liberal, more collectivist polyarchy" (pp. 166, 345–48). Under existing polyarchy, "vetoes are widely distributed," so that "opponents of any positive policy to cope with a problem can obstruct it" (p. 346). Although this wide distribution of vetoes was established to protect the rights of property against groups demanding a redistribution of income or wealth, such "distributional issues" are now, says Lindblom, less important than the "collective problems" of energy, environment and economic stability. "The emerging peril to the survival of polyarchy," he says, "is that vetoes are increasingly cast not simply against proposed redistribution but against proposed solutions to collective problems" (p. 347). Hence Lindblom concludes that mutual adjustment in existing polyarchies should be restructured so that policies addressing these problems cannot be vetoed by the private or corporate interests the policies adversely affect.

Lindblom is less specific in his description of collectivist polyarchy than he is in his discussion of planner sovereignty markets, but he does provide a few suggestions about how collectivist polyarchy might be structured. Generally, he argues it would resemble the market, in the sense that innovation of policies would be encouraged but vetoes would be limited. Specifically, he says that planning and policy making in collectivist polyarchy would resemble the wartime planning and policy making of existing polyarchies, where the economy is highly organized through direct government purchases (planner sovereignty markets), but where a wide range of personal liberties are protected.[5]

Criticisms and Rejoinders

Like many peacemakers who are attacked by the very parties they are trying to mediate, Lindblom's efforts to develop a position that combines the insights of liberalism and Marxism have been met with criticisms from both theoretical camps.

From the Marxists

From the Marxist camp, Lindblom has been challenged by John Manley, who in an article in the *American Political Science Review* takes both Lindblom and his one-time collaborator, Robert Dahl, to task for trying to salvage pluralism rather than moving on to a thoroughly Marxist analysis emphasizing social class. Manley argues that Lindblom's (and Dahl's) position has a serious internal contradiction and is also incorrect in its conclusions about power relations in the United States.

The internal inconsistency with which Manley charges Lindblom concerns incrementalism. Manley says that Lindblom advocates making incremental changes to public policy, as opposed to large-scale "structural" reforms, and yet that Lindblom also calls for a fundamental alteration of the U.S. political economy. How, asks Manley, are we to revolutionize the system while making only incremental changes?

With respect to Lindblom's analysis of power, Manley argues that Lindblom does not pay enough attention to the important role played by *economic* inequality in perpetuating *political* inequality. In so doing, says Manley, Lindblom is led to recommend political reforms that, from Manley's perspective, (a) will never be adopted, because capitalists are able to prevent the reforms from even being considered; and (b), even if they were adopted, would not promote equality because they would leave ownership of corporations in private hands. Manley concludes that

> inequality under capitalism is not a by-product of the system that is amenable to polyarchal corrections. It is a structural impera- tive. It is one of the things that makes capitalism capitalism and distinguishes it from socialism. From the class perspective, in- equality is as likely to be significantly reduced or eliminated under capitalism as the meek are to inherit the earth.

As Lindblom notes in his rejoinder to Manley (in Lindblom, 1983), Manley's critique is insightful, but it misses the mark on many important points because it confuses Lindblom's theoretical strategy in *Politics and Markets* with some of his positions in earlier works. Manley's confusion about incrementalism is revealed in a statement that he makes almost offhandedly. Incrementalism, he says, "by definition ensures at best slow changes in the status quo" (p. 380). Actually, by "incrementalism" Lindblom means simply a series of small adjustments, not necessarily that the changes are unthreatening to the existing order. He has made this point elsewhere (Lindblom, 1979), but it is particularly relevant to *Politics and Markets*. In the latter, he is claiming that very small changes at key points—that is, small changes in politico-economic mechanisms—can cause major changes in the competition of ideas, free up volitions, and lead to radical changes in policy. Another way of saying this is to point out that what is considered to be a funda- mental change depends on one's assumptions. By 'fundamental,' Manley means nationalizing the modes of production. But for Lind- blom this would actually produce a very constrained competition of ideas and a very conservative, repressive government. In Lind- blom's view, minor extensions of political control over the econ- omy, if correctly targeted, could drastically expand the system's openness and flexibility.

By the same token, Lindblom's theory suggests that Manley's emphasis on social class is misdirected. Manley claims that Lind- blom conceptualizes the problem of inequality in terms of public opinion. In a sense, Manley is correct, but he fails to see that Lindblom traces the public's willingness to accept inequality to structural features of capitalism and to the lopsided competition of ideas that these features produce (on this point, see Lindblom, 1983, p. 386). "We need to caution ourselves," Lindblom says, "against overestimating the effect of class in retarding a fuller democracy" (p. 355). The more important barrier is "the autonomy of the private corporation," and in theory this barrier can be obviated with a collectivist polyarchy and a planner sovereignty market system.

From the Liberals

From the theorists in favor of more or less unrestrained capitalism, Lindblom has been criticized indirectly in a recent book by Peter L. Berger (1986). Berger presents a number of propositions that challenge Lindblom's thesis that politico-economic mechanisms can be combined in an almost unlimited variety of ways. Berger claims, to the contrary, that capitalism and liberal democracy on the one hand, and socialism and totalitarianism on the other hand, are two distinct forms of society with little if any middle ground between them. From Berger's perspective the term "democratic socialism" is an oxymoron, like "circular square" or "macho femininity" (Berger, p. 226).

The basis for this conclusion is Berger's premise that minor reductions in business autonomy lead, in a sudden burst or qualitative shift, to a totalitarian government. Whereas Lindblom sees the possibility of many gradations in the balance between the government and business, Berger claims that once one moves from limited government to even modest forms of public ownership of business, the government-business balance tilts rapidly toward government (p. 79):

Whatever else socialism may mean as a utopian vision, *empirically* it has consistently meant an immense expansion of state power, indeed amounting to a quantum leap of this power. ... The political controls over the economy dictated by the socialist project must be, by their very nature, permanently insti-

tutionalized; thus they are very difficult to relax (let alone remove) once established. Put differently, empirical socialism has
meant a pervasive bureaucratization of the economy; quite apart
from the economic malfunctions this brings about (malfunctions
that go a very long way in explaining the low efficiency of
socialist economies), the all-embracing bureaucracy makes the
expression of political liberties very difficult if not impossible.

From this, Berger concludes (p. 81) that "capitalism is a necessary
but not sufficient condition for democracy."

Berger is also very skeptical of the possibility envisioned by
Lindblom of equalizing wealth and income. Berger's view (pp.
50–55) is that all societies will inevitably be stratified or ranked by
some criterion or other. Capitalist societies are stratified almost exclusively by wealth and income. Socialist societies simply add onto
this criterion an additional ranking based on political connections.
Thus, rather than leading to equality, socialism makes *in*equality ar-
bitrary—subject not to merit but to cronyism.

Berger's arguments about the impossibility of democratic socialism and equality rest on a theory of power. He believes that all
social systems are stratified and more or less centrally controlled.
From his perspective all groups seek to expand their privileges and
benefits, and power depends mainly on who wins in these struggles.

This view of power is similar to Lindblom's, except that it does
not include a role for the public in the struggle between contending
groups. Consequently, in response to Berger, Lindblom would
probably say that the power of elites depends not simply or even
primarily on their competitions with each other but on the willingness of the larger population to accept their leadership. In turn, the
public's conception of its political options depends on the scope of
ideas to which they are exposed, a scope that is tilted one way or the
other as a function of politico-economic mechanisms. In support of
his position, Lindblom could point to the fragility of power—to the
way that it can dissolve as soon as people change their minds.
Consider the fall of the Shah of Iran, or for an example closer to
home, the collapse of the Reagan administration's power after the

Iran-Contra disclosures. In short, Berger sees power as resting on coercion and direct group-to-group conflict, whereas Lindblom concludes that it involves the mass public and rests largely on persuasion.

Of course, the proof of the theory is in the evidence. Berger and Manley as well as Lindblom are making empirical claims about the effects of certain changes in public policy. To some extent we can use the Great Society to judge Lindblom's thesis that politico-economic mechanisms determine the nature of politics and public debate.

Chapter 5
Political Impacts of a
Change in Property Rights

LINDBLOM'S THEORY provides a template for identify-
ing effects of the Great Society that the other theories thus far considered have overlooked, and it also offers some reinterpretations of
impacts that we have already examined. In arguing that the relationship between government and business determines the nature of
politics in different political-economic systems, Lindblom implies
that fundamental social change can be achieved by making minor
alterations to politico-economic mechanisms. Thus the theory calls
for the Great Society to be scrutinized for any changes it made in
the relationship between business and government, and it directs
attention to the effects these changes may have had on public
debate and popular demands.

Lindblom's Explanation of
Poverty

An explanation of poverty in America flows implicitly from
Lindblom's analysis of private enterprise polyarchy. For purposes
of clarification, figure 5-1 illustrates Lindblom's conception of
polyarchic systems. The persuasion system is placed at the bottom
of the figure, with the economic and political systems above it, to
depict Lindblom's thesis that the competition of ideas between top
leaders in business and government shapes public opinion. The persuasion system is conceptualized as a process of information diffusion, where individuals form volitions and complex judgments on
the basis of their preferences, irrational drives, and morals on the
one hand and the information they receive from the economic and
political systems on the other.[1] (Lindblom's analysis of volitions is
found in *Politics and Markets*, pp. 201–21.) Other things being

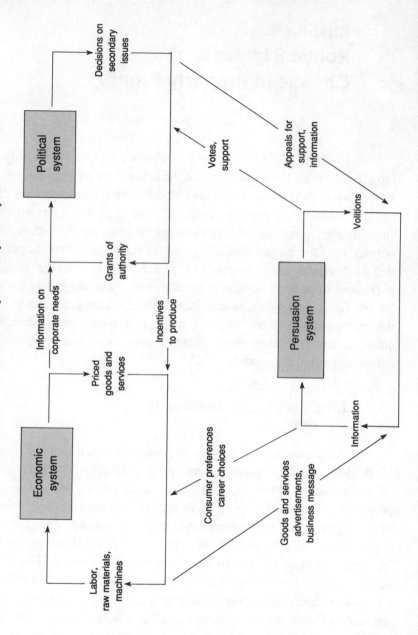

Figure 5-1. Lindblom's Conception of Polyarchic Systems

equal, information governs action. Because the range of alternative policies debated in the political system is limited to what leaders in business find acceptable, the information available to the public about policy options is restricted to "secondary issues," and people's volitions are thereby constrained.

Lindblom's explanation of poverty begins from an assumption that labor markets in private enterprise economies, unless modified by taxes and other redistributive devices, automatically generate a pool of impoverished workers, a pool that contracts and expands cyclically (Lindblom, 1977, pp. 37–51, 82–84). When producers are selling their products at an acceptable price, they expand production to increase their earnings, hire more workers, and thus reduce the ranks of the unemployed. Eventually, however, the expansion of production depletes the pool of unemployed workers to the point that wages, bid up in the competition between employers for available labor, rise and cut into profits. Unable to make an acceptable return on their investments, employers curtail production, and the pool of unemployed workers expands. Economic growth does not begin anew until wage demands fall in response to the abundance of labor. Necessarily, those workers who remain unemployed most or all of the time through the cycle are poor.

Lindblom argues that the solution to the problem of poverty is straightforward: simply redistribute income from the rich to the poor as often as is necessary to maintain greater equality. Disposable income can be "wholly equalized" through taxation without a resultant decline in productivity because "high-income people are more motivated by the 'scores' they make—their pretax income —than by the actual disposable income they receive" (p. 44). From this perspective poverty is a political, not an economic problem. In Lindblom's words (p. 44):

> Historically, all societies, market or not, have preserved economic inequality. The barrier to economic and wealth equality in real-world market-oriented systems is not any internal logic. It is instead ... a historically inherited and politically maintained inequality in individual assets, earning power, and income

shares. . , . In principle, governments can redistribute income and
wealth and repeat the redistribution as frequently as wished.
Their disinclination to do so requires a political explanation
rather than reference to market forces.

As we have seen, Lindblom's "political explanation" focuses on the
politico-economic mechanisms of private enterprise polyarchies.
Because of the privileged position of business in these systems,
government leaders and the public are led to believe through a lopsided competition of ideas that redistributing income would undermine liberty, individual initiative, popular control of government,
and economic efficiency. Income redistribution and other primary
issues are kept off the public agenda.

Adding to the "circularity" of politics in the private enterprise
polyarchies are the additional effects of class indoctrination. People
think and act differently in the lower class because they are treated
differently by teachers, judges, police officers, and even their economic peers. In Lindblom's words (p. 225):

> One study after another has documented the phenomenon
> that school teachers are more helpful to students perceived to be
> of middle to upper class than lower class, that school resources
> go more generously to upper classes, and that upper classes are
> presumed to need tracking into schools or curricula suited to
> their classes. The same studies and others show that parental
> treatment of children encourages greater independence, imagina-
> tion, self-confidence, and resourcefulness in middle to upper
> class children. The many studies just cited on schooling and
> rearing of children show that habits of obedience to authority and
> of deference are instilled into children of the less favored classes.
> The judicial system is harsher in arrest, detention, and sentencing
> with lower class than with middle to upper.

Lindblom's theory provides little hope that the poor themselves
will see through the business message. His conception of volitions
assumes that an individual's will is shaped largely by the range of

options communicated to him in the competition of ideas. Because in the polyarchies primary issues are suppressed, the poor will never be able to break out of their fettered imaginations on their own. The problem of poverty, along with other problems that cannot be solved without restrictions on corporate autonomy, will remain as long as the system's politico-economic mechanisms leave business with inordinate authority.

Analysis of Policy Impacts

.Lindblom's theory points to two different types of research on the Great Society. First, his analysis of the relationship between politico-economic mechanisms and public opinion suggests that the changes made by the Great Society in the relationship between business and government should have had far-reaching impacts on public debate, politics, and public opinion. In this regard, the theory directs our attention especially to the Civil Rights Act of 1964, which comes close to what Lindblom has in mind with planner sovereignty markets. Initially, the act was very weak because it required that discrimination be proved, but in the late 1960s it was modified by a series of Executive Orders to require affirmative action by all federal contractors. Federal contractors were made to develop a plan showing numerical objectives for integrating their work force and to take actions assuring that the objectives were approached. In this way, the burden of proof was shifted from protected minorities to the employers themselves; the employers had to show action, rather than the job applicants or workers having to show discrimination. In effect, this redefined property rights and shifted the balance of control over labor markets away from business and toward government.

The second research strategy implied by Lindblom's theory is to reexamine the impacts of social action. Lindblom's conception of poverty differs from those of the cultural theory of poverty and the theory of welfare dependency in that it rejects the thesis that the peculiar beliefs and behaviors of the poor derive from their immediate circumstances. In Lindblom's view, the commonly ob-

served characteristics of poor people stem from "class indoctrination." From this perspective, the impacts of social action need to be
reexamined for any indication that the poverty culture is coming
from agents of socialization in the larger society rather than from
"carriers" of the poverty culture in the poor communities themselves.

The Effects of Civil Rights

Given the dramatic effects that civil rights laws have had in
this country, it is amazing how little attention is now paid to them
in debates over the Great Society and the Reagan Revolution. The
tendency has been for both sides in the argument to assume that
civil rights issues have been resolved and to want to move on, as it
were, to the more controversial and pressing issues surrounding income and in-kind transfers. Admittedly, the Reagan administration
launched some forays against affirmative action, but in large part
they came to naught. Policy makers seem to have concluded that the
battle over equality of opportunity has been won, even if the war on
poverty was lost, and no one, except those on the extreme right,
wants to fight the battle again.

The impacts of civil rights laws actually deserve much more
attention than this because they raise serious questions about both
the cultural theory of poverty and the theory of welfare dependency.
As previously stated (in chapter 2), in less than a decade the Voting
Rights Act led to massive increases in black voting and political
representation, and the Civil Rights Act, coupled with grants and
loans for higher education, produced rapid gains in black education,
employment, and earnings. Obviously, if the poor have a culture
that is resistant to change and that is characterized by short time
horizons and limited ability to defer gratification, such dramatic and
immediate effects should never have occurred. Regardless of
whether one assumes that the culture comes from isolation or instead from "familial anarchy," the expectation would be that
changes in political, economic, and educational patterns would not
occur overnight. Presumably, new opportunities for the poor would
go unused, unless, first, the poor were somehow resocialized.

Lindblom's theory implies that civil rights laws were effective because they altered the system's political mechanisms. In theory, the poor do not have a poverty culture that is resistant to change; they have class-specific attitudes that are created and maintained through indoctrination.

A person's opportunities, and his perceptions of the costs and benefits associated with them, are the sole pathways of his imagination. A small change from civil rights laws in access to work, power, and education led to quick and far-reaching changes in behavior because, *ex hypothesi,* the options available to the poor were expanded and their volitions changed accordingly. Thus Lindblom's theory is consistent with a major finding from the Great Society that the other theories under consideration seem unable to explain.

There is, though, a fallback position for those who hold to either the culture of poverty theory or the theory of welfare dependency. It might be that the observed impacts of the Great Society on racial equality had very little to do with the hard-core poor. Certainly it can be argued that many American blacks in the 1960s had middle-class abilities even though they earned only poverty wages. Prior to the Civil Rights Act, black college graduates had few options besides teaching in the public schools, and high school graduates had fewer options still. Perhaps qualified blacks whose wages and political opportunities had long been held down artificially by discrimination were simply given opportunities and incomes commensurate with their education and ability. If so, the hypothesis from Lindblom's theory that structural changes altered the beliefs and attitudes of the poor might be inaccurate.

Policy research on the Great Society never examined the effects of civil rights laws on the attitudes of blacks and other minorities. We have no way of knowing whether in 1964 most blacks had short time horizons and limited ability to defer gratification, or what effects changes in economic, educational, and political opportunities had on their beliefs and volitions. Consequently, it is impossible to determine, at least in any direct way, which of the theories—Lindblom's, the Great Society's, or the Reagan Revolution's—is correct on this issue.

The only way around this gap in the data is to consider the argument that Lindblom makes about the effects of politico-economic mechanisms on politics and public opinion. At least three findings from the Great Society are required to support Lindblom's thesis that expansions of planner sovereignty markets have the impacts that he claims for them: (1) civil rights laws must have had direct effects on the practices of employers in economic sectors where planner sovereignty markets were used to promote equality of opportunity; (2) changes in property rights must have altered public opinion about policy on racial issues; and (3) changes in attitudes about racial policy must have spilled over into other areas of public opinion. In other words, the redefinition of property rights under civil rights laws must be shown to have expanded minority opportunities, which in turn must be found to have expanded the range of alternatives debated in politics and perceived by the public.

Although largely ignored by conservative critics of the Great Society, there is evidence from policy research that the strategy of planner sovereignty markets was effective in altering employer behavior. A study by Ashenfelter and Heckman (1973) compared the hiring practices of federal contractors, who, as previously stated, were covered by affirmative action requirements, to those of other private employers who had no such obligations. Between 1966 and 1970, companies with federal contracts expanded their employment of black males by 3.3 percent more than companies without federal funding. Similarly, during the same time frame, the share of total wages going to black workers in firms with federal contracts increased 3 percent more than the total share of wages of black workers in other firms. The exact way in which these impacts were produced is not known. It could have been through "tokenism" or through improved techniques for locating qualified blacks or by some other mechanism altogether. The important point is that, as Lindblom's theory would have led us to expect, the immediate effects of civil rights laws on minority employment and income appear to have been concentrated among federal contractors.

Changes in the public's racial attitudes during the years of the

Great Society have also been documented. Table 5-1 shows the percentage of liberal responses from U.S. whites on a number of race-related questions asked in 1963, 1972, and 1977. On every issue there was an increase in tolerance, and on four out five issues the increase was dramatic. Additional opinion data (not shown) reveal that between 1963 and 1977 the greatest shift in attitudes occurred in the South, where racial prejudice had been common for several hundred years (Condran, 1979; Sheatsley, 1966). From Lindblom's perspective this means simply that, as his theory would have suggested, a change in policy led to a change in attitudes. Apparently, contrary to popular belief, morality can indeed be legislated.

Finally, there is also evidence to suggest that after the Civil Rights Act was passed in 1964 other groups in addition to blacks began to see government as responsible for their position in society and to believe that additional civil rights interventions were needed. The civil rights movement for racial equality was followed by similar movements from women, homosexuals, native Americans, and senior citizens. Similarly, there was a successful push by the handicapped for policies to facilitate their access to public facilities, education, and employment. Today, in stark contrast to the years preceding the Great Society, America is very sensitive to assuring equality of opportunity to many minorities, not blacks alone.

Of course, none of this evidence shows conclusively that Lindblom is correct in his argument that the balance between government and business determines the scope and nature of politics and public opinion. All we have done is to verify some key points in the causal chain implied by Lindblom's theory. The linkages between these points have not been examined, and hence the analysis rests heavily on speculation and inference. Nevertheless, were it not for Lindblom's theory we would have ignored some of the most profound social and political changes associated with the Great Society. Although it seems far removed from everyday politics, Lindblom's treatise on the world's political-economic systems has opened our eyes to the possibility that the impacts of antipoverty policy extend well beyond the poverty population.

Table 5-1. Percent "Liberal" for Five Racial Attitudes,
U.S. Whites, 1963, 1972, and 1977

	1963 (%)	1972 (%)	1977 (%)
Do you think that white students and Negro students should go to the same schools or separate schools?	63	86	86
How strongly would you object if a member of your family wanted to bring a Negro friend home to dinner?	50	70	71
Do you think there should be laws against marriages between Negroes and Whites?	36	61	72
White people have a right to keep Negroes out of their neighborhoods if they want to, and Negroes should respect that right.	39	60	58
Negroes shouldn't push themselves where they're not wanted.	22	24	27

Source: John G. Condran, "Changes in White Attitudes Toward Blacks: 1963–1977," *Public Opinion Quarterly*, 43 (Winter 1979): 463–76. Adapted from table 1, p. 466.

Social Action

Lindblom's theory also offers a new slant on the results of social action programs. As discussed previously (in chapter 3), the temporariness of the impacts of compensatory education, occupational skills training, and community organization programs leave little doubt that there are forces acting on the poor to make them think and act in a certain way. Both the cultural theory of poverty and the theory of welfare dependency assume that the poor's short time horizons and orientation to immediate gratification come from a culture that is localized within poor people's immediate communities. The two theories disagree only about where this community-specific culture comes from in the first place. One theory traces it to isolation from mainstream institutions, the other to the dominance of single, separated, and divorced males in poor neighborhoods.

In contrast, Lindblom's theory suggests that the so-called poverty culture, while unique to the lower class, is part and parcel of the political-economic system as a whole. In theory, individuals in different social classes are constantly being indoctrinated to behave and to think in accord with their position in the social hierarchy. The poor often use their limited incomes to buy fancy clothes and flashy cars because they, like everyone else, are led to emulate the rich. Conversely, the poor speak, act, and think differently from the rest of society because they are treated with disdain by teachers, police officers, sales clerks, and other authority figures with whom they come into contact. This conception of the poverty culture leads to a reinterpretation of the findings from policy research on social action.

The most important evidence from compensatory education is no longer that the initial gains in learning dissipated after participants left the program. All the theories under consideration would have led us to predict, or at least would allow us to account for, this finding. More significant from the perspective offered by Lindblom is that compensatory education, while ineffective in permanently enhancing learning achievement, had lasting effects on the participants' future choices regarding school and careers. As previously stated, participants were more likely than nonparticipants with similar backgrounds to complete high school and to enter college, and less likely to be arrested or to have other problems (Berrueta-Clement, 1984). This "halo effect" suggests that compensatory education programs altered the participants' volitions by bringing them into contact with authority figures (teachers) genuinely committed to their later success. At the same time, this finding also challenges the thesis from the culture of poverty and welfare dependency theories that people in poor communities—be they parents or "flamboyant youths"—are the main carriers and transmitters of the poverty culture. As Lindblom argues, teachers and, by extension, other authority figures in the surrounding society appear to play a crucial role in shaping the decisions and ambitions of poor children.

A similar approach can be taken in interpreting the evidence from research on occupational skills training. Again, the temporariness of gains in employment and earnings from these programs would be attributed by the culture of poverty and welfare dependency theories to the counteracting effects of the poverty culture. The hypothesis is that the poor can be removed from their environment and motivated to work, but once they leave the program and return to normal life in their communities, they go back to their original pattern of periodic employment. The problem with this hypothesis is that it ignores the finding of lasting wage and employment gains among new entrants into the labor force. Why do training programs prove effective for the inexperienced but of little value to workers who have already been employed? If the culture of poor communities is washing out the motivational effects of training programs, then why are these effects *not* washed out among program participants who are making their initial entrance into the world of work?

Lindblom's conception of the economy offers a simple explanation for this apparent anomaly. Older workers have already gained the rudimentary skills provided by training programs, and hence the programs give them no lasting advantage in the labor market compared to other workers with similar experience. On the other hand, new entrants into the labor market benefit from such programs precisely because they are starting with fewer skills. To explain the impacts of occupational skills training, there is no need to fall back onto a thesis about the pathological culture of poor communities. The training was simply of use only to those who had never worked.

Finally, Lindblom's theory also implies an alternative interpretation for the direction taken by Community Action Agencies. Few analysts have paid much attention to the Community Action Program, but when we look at this program through Lindblom's eyes, it takes on considerable importance. Neither the cultural theory of poverty nor the theory of welfare dependency sees the political system as an organization with its own interest. The rationale for CAAs was the premise that government responds to organized interests and produces decisions that reflect the balance of interests surrounding it. This same premise has led recently to a similar program for organizing business as an interest group in federal social programs. Private Industry Councils have been established throughout the United States in an effort to make employment and training programs more responsive to the private sector.[2] Policy makers continue to believe that government is a passive agency, a weather vane that turns with the shifting winds of organized pressure.

In contrast, Lindblom's theory assumes that leaders in government are motivated to protect and where possible to extend their authority as far as they can. From this perspective, the action taken by city governments in response to the Community Action Program is instructive. Rather than shifting their policies to accommodate the newly organized CAAs, the nation's mayors turned to the central government and demanded that federal monies be routed not directly to CAAs but indirectly through urban governments. Once federal dollars started flowing through the hands of locally elected officials, community action in its original form ceased to exist.

Thus, when we examine compensatory education, occupational skills training, and community action while entertaining Lindblom's conception of private enterprise polyarchies, we are led to reevaluate some of the conclusions reached earlier when all we had to work with were the culture of poverty and welfare dependency theories. A number of findings that initially seemed insignificant now take on new meaning. The effects of compensatory education on the future choices of program participants suggest that authority figures rather than residents of poor communities may actually be transmitting the poverty culture. The success of training programs in raising the earnings and enhancing the employment of new entrants into the labor force casts doubt on the thesis that the low incomes of poor people reflect their weak orientation to work rather than the limited skills they have to offer in exchange for a livelihood. And the reaction of the political system to the Community Action Program suggests that government may not be as passive and responsive as policy makers on both the right and the left often assume. Overall, the findings from policy research on social action seem now to indicate that the poverty culture actually has its roots not in poor communities but in the larger society.

Challenges to Lindblom

Although Lindblom's theory is thus able to account for many findings from policy research on the Great Society that otherwise would have gone unnoticed, the theory is not without anomalies. There is at least one area where the effects of the Great Society raise questions about Lindblom's call for income redistribution. Lindblom states explicitly that redistributions of income will not undermine work motives, and yet there is a sizable body of research showing just the opposite. How might Lindblom respond to this evidence in defense of his argument that income redistribution is the appropriate approach for reducing poverty?

One counterargument is that Lindblom's thesis about work motives is about high-income individuals rather than about the poor. His actual words were (p. 44):

> Empirical evidence reveals no clear association between degrees of income inequality and differences in work habits, or diligence. . . . [The more egalitarian market] systems of Scandinavia, for example, do not show productivity losses when compared with the relatively more inegalitarian United States. Nor can we find in responses to decades of increasingly severe income taxation evidence of declining managerial incentives. . . . This evidence supports the hypothesis that high-income people are more motivated by the "scores" they make—their pretax income—than by the actual disposable income they receive. Such a hypothesis opens up the revolutionary possibility that a market-oriented system might preserve work incentives through "scoreboard" incomes even though taxation wholly equalized disposable income.

Although this argument is attractive, it fails to deal with the issue raised by the Reagan administration. The Reagan view is not that "managerial incentives" have declined or that income redistribution undermines the work motives of the middle class. Rather, the administration is concerned that welfare undermines the work motives of the poor and breaks up poor families. Furthermore, the finding that welfare reduces labor force entry seems to challenge Lindblom's claim that class indoctrination maintains work motives even in the face of weak market incentives.

A stronger counterargument to the Reagan view is that the income and in-kind transfers of the Great Society were not the kind of income redistribution that Lindblom's theory implies is needed. Lindblom's approach requires that an equitable distribution of income be part of a larger reduction in business privileges and a corresponding expansion of employment opportunities. Not welfare but jobs with security and decent pay are the kinds of income redistribution that Lindblom has in mind. The transfers of the Great Society were provided as handouts. In-kind transfers of medicine, food, and housing required that recipients identify themselves as poor when they paid their bills, thus further indoctrinating them to see themselves as failures rather than the system as unfair. Similarly, to obtain transfers of income the poor had to submit to a humiliating process of eligibility determination that was often designed to discourage participation. Hence, given Lindblom's theory, the income and in-kind transfers of the Great Society reinforced existing class attitudes.

Moreover, the fact that welfare reduces the propensity to work can be reconciled with the view that volitions depend on preferences and perceived opportunities. The poor often choose government-subsidized leisure over gainful employment because the employment opportunities available to them offer little income, long hours, and no potential for advancement. Withdrawing from the labor force and going on the dole may actually satisfy more preferences than working long and hard for low pay. The way around this problem, Lindblom would probably say, is not to follow the dictates of the "business message" and cut welfare for the needy, but to guide the production process so as to assure that available jobs are worth having.

Clearly, this line of reasoning, like those discussed with regard to civil rights laws and social action programs, points to some potentially promising strategies for research. The approach used by most policy analysts in evaluating income transfers was to assess the extent to which transfers reduce labor force entry. The alternative approach implied above would be to examine the effects not of transfers alone but of transfers in the context of employment opportunities. If Lindblom's theory is correct, welfare is a disincentive to work only when job opportunities are limited.

An important study bears directly on this argument: it is Goodwin's detailed analysis (1972) of the work motives of welfare recipients. Goodwin's research findings indicate that the attitudes of the poor are caused by work experiences rather than the reverse. Goodwin administered detailed written questionnaires to several samples: long-term AFDC mothers and their sons; short-term welfare mothers and sons; black fathers, mothers, and sons who were members of working families and who lived in the suburbs or "outer city"; male and female members of white families who lived in the same neighborhoods as the outer-city blacks; teenagers from an almost all-black neighborhood in Washington, D.C.; and welfare recipients enrolled in the Work Incentive Program (WIN), a job training program designed to move people off welfare. Although in most cases Goodwin's research was cross-sectional rather than longitudinal (only the WIN sample was re-interviewed), the use of a variety of samples allowed him to draw conclusions about the relationship between attitudes and experience.

Goodwin found no basic differences in the goals and values of the poor and nonpoor with respect to work. The poor people examined in his study were just as likely as the nonpoor to want to work and to see work as important to self-esteem. The poor differed from the nonpoor only in lacking confidence in their ability to succeed, and this lack of confidence appeared to stem from actual work failures rather than from some sort of class-based pessimism. WIN participants who terminated training without finding employment showed a decline in confidence, an expanded propensity to see welfare as acceptable, and a reduction in efforts to find employment. In turn, poor mothers transmitted their lack of confidence to their sons, who, although no less likely to work than other people, tended to terminate schooling earlier than sons from more confident homes. Goodwin summarized his findings as follows (pp. 112–13):

Evidence from this study unambiguously supports the following conclusion: poor people—males and females, blacks and whites, youths and adults—identify their self-esteem with work as strongly as do the nonpoor. They express as much willingness to take job training if unable to earn a living and to work even if they were to have an adequate income. . . . [They have], moreover, as high life aspirations as do the nonpoor and want the same things, among them a good education and a nice place to live. . . . If poor persons, especially welfare recipients, really regard work as important for their self-esteem, why are they not working and moving out of poverty? . . . The picture that emerges is one of black welfare women who want to work but who, because of continuing failure in the work world, tend to become more accepting of welfare and less inclined to try again.

Thus the research by Goodwin supports Lindblom's view of class attitudes and raises doubts about both the cultural theory of poverty and the theory of welfare dependency. It appears that, while the poor do indeed have limited abilities and some peculiar attitudes, their so-called culture comes not from isolation from "mainstream institutions" or from the prevalence of "flamboyant youths" in their communities, but rather from their limited economic opportunities and their failures in the world of work.

Chapter 6
Habermas's *Legitimation Crisis*

ALTHOUGH LINDBLOM's theory expands the scope of our inquiry, it still perpetuates one of the analytical limitations inherent in the prevailing approach to policy research. Specifically, Lindblom does not take us beyond the usual emphasis of policy analysis on policy *impacts* as opposed to policy *formulation*. In most policy research, the issues leading up to a policy, the interests that articulate these issues, and the openness or bias in the process where a policy is selected, are excluded from consideration. Program components are treated as independent variables in a causal chain, not as decisions that were reached via procedures that warrant evaluation. Although Lindblom directs our attention to the changes the Great Society made in politico-economic mechanisms and to the effects of these changes on public opinion, it does not extend our investigation to how the Great Society was developed in the first place.

The restriction of policy analysis to policy impacts is based implicitly on a cognitive-instrumental conception of rationality. As with the thesis of situational determinism, policy analysts appear to have drawn this model of reasoning unknowingly, or at least uncritically, from premises implicit in U.S. public policy. In both the Great Society and the Reagan Revolution, it was assumed that people have pre-existing preferences, which they seek to satisfy in the most direct and complete way possible given their understanding of their options. The Great Society was designed to change the behavior of the poor by giving them basic necessities so that they would shift their attention from day-to-day survival to opportunities further out in time. Similarly, the Reagan Revolution attempted to influence the behavior of the poor by altering the economic incentives and disincentives surrounding them. In both cases, the reasoning process of the poor was conceptualized as one of identifying pathways to given ends, calculating the expenditures of resources and probabilities of success associated with each one, and choosing the action that would assure success with the least cost.

Lindblom's theory holds to a similar model of rationality; it simply shifts the source of the individual's perceptions of his opportunities from immediate circumstances to the information received from a competition of ideas among top leaders. This move allows Lindblom to treat property rights and political procedures as "politico-economic mechanisms" that are separate from and, in a causal sense, prior to public opinion. In theory, changes in the mechanisms cause changes in the scope of ideas considered in the debate among elites, and this alters people's perceptions of their options and causes changes in their volitions.

A cognitive-instrumental conception of rationality leads analysts to ignore policy formulation because it implies that the ways in which policies are formulated have no bearing on their effects. Since, in theory, people focus almost exclusively on their perceived opportunities, what matters in politics is the effects of new laws or government transfers on people's perceptions of their options, not how the laws or transfer programs were arrived at. The development of public policy can thus be split off conceptually, and policy analysis can be restricted to the identification of behavioral or attitudinal "impacts."

Habermas provides us with new insights into the Great Society because he conceives of reason as a process not of choosing pathways to given ends but of reaching understanding in a social context. This shifts the analytic focus to policy formulation.

Principles of Organization

Habermas believes that societies are organized ultimately not by exchange or command but through communication and voluntarily accepted norms. In his view, although norms are not always developed through explicit discussions and argumentation, they derive their powerful social influence from the expectation that they could be discursively justified if the need were to arise. Norms have a binding character—people believe they ought to obey them—because people believe they could be convinced that the norms are appropriate or "right."

Central to Habermas's theory is a distinction between action and discourse (White, 1979). Action involves an ongoing exchange of statements where implicit cognitive and normative assumptions remain unarticulated and unquestioned. Conversely, in discourse, action is suspended and problematic assumptions are explicated and debated.

Habermas argues that an expectation of discourse is built into the communicative foundations of social organization and that it operates as an emancipatory force in history. In speaking to each other, human beings presuppose that they hold beliefs, intentionally follow norms, and could give reasons for their norms and values if asked to. Thus, in relying on speech to coordinate their activity, people presuppose that if there is a disagreement about how to proceed, it will be resolved through discourse. This idea is emancipatory because it contains a radically democratic model of social coordination, one where norms are developed through discussion among free and equal people who are oriented exclusively to a search for the truth.

Of course, Habermas recognizes that large parts of modern societies are coordinated without recourse to communicative processes for reaching agreement, and he admits that in these spheres of action a cognitive-instrumental conception of rationality rather than one of communicative reason applies. However, he claims that the separating out of action areas itself has a communicative foundation. Although production is organized through exchange rather than consensus, the market system rests on people's conviction that private enterprise is desirable. Similarly, modern government directs people's behavior by issuing commands, but its power is not freestanding; it is anchored in the belief that authority flows from the citizenry. Habermas argues that these premises about economics and politics were developed historically through discourse and that today they can be discursively challenged.

In *Legitimation Crisis* Habermas presents a model of history that links the evolution of political and economic organization to the development of specialized forms of discourse. He argues that social systems have evolved through a series of "principles of organization" that govern production and institutionalize discourse on particular topics. He identifies two types of discourse that have been institutionalized thus far in history: practical reason and technical reason. (For a detailed discussion of Habermas's epistemology, see Keat, 1981.)[1] Practical reason deals with human norms and values, and, historically, it is the first form of discourse to emerge and be split off from informal communication. In opposition to positivist philosophies of science that claim that norms have no rational foundation, Habermas argues that ethical principles are developed through real or hypothetical discussions that test the generalizability of social rules. In contrast, technical reason develops knowledge of nature by testing empirical assumptions against conditional predictions. It is this learning process that has been institutionalized in modern societies and that, according to Habermas, has fostered the widespread belief in a cognitive-instrumental model of rationality.

Habermas places his own theory in a third category: critical reason. Critical reason explicates the presuppositions of communicative action and then assesses existing discourse against these premises. Communication distortions and blockages are identified by tracking arguments back to their foundations. Habermas believes that this analytical process can serve as a midwife to a new social order where the promise of unrestricted communication is institutionalized.

Habermas presents his model of how societies shift from one principle of organization to another as a theory of political crisis.[2] He suggests that the process, while actually characterized by turmoil, false starts, and regressions, can be reconstructed as a three-stage development. First, the social system begins encountering problems that cannot be solved by the existing learning mechanism.

Ruling classes try to deal with these problems, but their efforts only reveal the system's limitations. Second, a new social class emerges and draws on the discursive promise inherent in speech to develop a set of moral and political principles that push beneath the communicative limitations of the prevailing reasoning process. Examples of such classes include the biblical prophets and the Calvinistic capitalists of the sixteenth and seventeenth centuries. Third, as systemic problems mount, the more advanced principles of these classes gradually begin to dominate and drive out their predecessors, and suppressed learning processes are released to deal with the problems the social system has encountered.

For our purposes, the most important argument Habermas makes is that people expect problematic norms to be debated and either justified or changed. In theory, history would have been characterized by a rapid development of technical and organizational capacity if it were not for the fact that dominant classes are threatened by the spread of discourse to new topics. Through a variety of means that historically have ranged from rituals and incantations in traditional societies to propaganda and policy sciences today, elites restrict discourse to topics that do not present immediate or potential challenges to their authority, and thus they short-circuit the communicative presupposition that norms will be reviewed discursively. Habermas's theory of political crisis is a theory of how this short circuit is overcome.

Social Formations

Habermas provides a table, here numbered 6-1, to clarify his view of history (*Legitimation Crisis,* p. 17). Primitive societies are the tribal societies of the Neolithic period, as well as the first settled cultures based on the domestication of animals and the cultivation of plants.[3] The category of traditional societies contains all precapitalist civilizations, including the Greek city-states, the Egyptian, Roman, and Chinese empires, and the feudal kingdoms of Europe. Habermas divides modern societies into capitalist societies and postcapitalist societies, the latter being "state socialist societies."[4] In analyzing crisis tendencies in capitalist societies, Habermas distinguishes between two stages of development: liberal capitalism, where there is little state intervention in the economy, and organized capitalism, where the state is actively involved in the capital accumulation process. Finally, *post*modern society is a theoretical possibility projected into the future.

Table 6-1. Social Formations

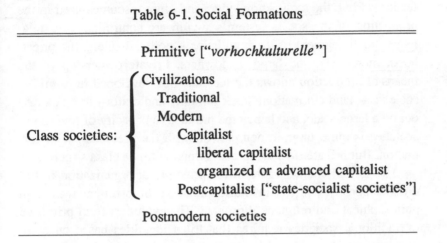

Primitive ["*vorhochkulturelle*"]

Class societies:
- Civilizations
  - Traditional
  - Modern
    - Capitalist
      - liberal capitalist
      - organized or advanced capitalist
    - Postcapitalist ["state-socialist societies"]

Postmodern societies

Crises in Earlier Social Formations

Habermas's analysis of social formations leading up to advanced capitalism lays the groundwork for his treatment of crisis tendencies in the present era. Essentially, he argues that the crises of earlier societies are due to the absence of learning processes that we now take for granted.

Primitive societies are organized around the primary roles of age and sex, and they have no institutionalized discourse. These societies develop mythological world views that, by explaining natural events with analogues from social relations, "interpret away" contingencies and counterbalance a lack of control over nature with "an illusion of order." Habermas argues that "it is external change that overloads the narrowly limited steering capacity of societies organized around kinship lines and undermines the familial and tribal identities" (p. 18). The most likely cause of crisis is overpopulation and land scarcity. In those societies that meet the evolutionary challenge, a judicial role is established to allow the societies to win a war or construct large irrigation projects, and this role becomes the core of a political subsystem.[5]

The institutionalization of a political subsystem marks the transition to a new principle of organization, which has two central features. First, the tools, knowledge, and other resources used in the production of the social system's wealth are controlled by a relatively small segment of the population—political rulers, the priesthood, merchants, and large landowners. Private ownership of the means of production allows the technologies developed in primitive societies—land cultivation, stock farming, and crafts—to be carried out on a large scale, and hence the productive capacity of traditional societies is quite large in comparison with the previous social formation. But private ownership also brings with it a class structure.

The second characteristic of the principle of organization in traditional societies is the institutionalization of practical reason in philosophical and religious discourse. The evolution from primitive to traditional societies requires that tribal identities based on common ancestry be replaced by more abstract identities based on belonging to a territorial organization. Although, initially, different tribal identities can be integrated through a polytheistic expansion of religion, this solution to the problem proves unstable, and the traditional societies that survive are those that develop "cosmologically grounded ethics, higher religions, and philosophies" (*Communication and the Evolution of Society*, p. 112).

Traditional societies collapse because their class structure and its supporting legal order are inconsistent with their legitimating religions, which cannot explicitly permit exploitation. Initially, this contradiction is suppressed from public consciousness. The "first principles" of the religion are removed from public argumentation and are immunized against objections, while the legal system is presented as "the legacy of an order of the world and of salvation that is posited absolutely" (*Communication and the Evolution of Society*, p. 112). However, in critical situations such as wars, traditional societies must expand production through heightened exploitation of labor, and this exposes the contradiction between the legal system and the religious ideology, causes people to question the prevailing religious and political principles, and leads to class struggles. Significantly, traditional societies cannot increase production by systematically developing new technologies because they cannot allow the institutionalization of technical reason; technical reason would undermine the traditions legitimating the legal order (*Toward a Rational Society*, pp. 94–96).

It is precisely this problem—the inability to increase production without generating class conflict—that the capitalist principle of organization overcomes. Under capitalism technical reason is institutionalized in science, and production is organized around competition between capitalists. New technologies are developed systematically because individual entrepreneurs make a profit by introducing labor-saving devices that allow them to undercut the prices of their competitors. Thus the market operates in cybernetic ways to promote increased productivity through technological innovation rather than, as in traditional society, through intensified exploitation of labor.

Capitalism would be an enduring social formation if it were not for the fact that economic problems arise that contradict the ideology justifying an independent economic subsystem. In the initial stages of capitalism when private enterprise is first being advocated, an "achievement ideology" arises; it claims that the economic system distributes income and wealth on the basis of initiative, ability, and effort. So long as this appears to be the case, the inequality associated with market systems is viewed as acceptable and natural. However, once economic depressions and mass unemployment begin to occur, people in the lower classes start to recognize that their situation, rather than being their own fault, is a consequence of the economic system, and they begin to agitate for change. Today, Habermas argues, it does not take exposure to Marxism for the population at large to recognize "that social force is exercised in the forms of economic exchange" (p. 81).

In response to these economic crises and the social movements they generate, the principle of organization in liberal capitalism is modified under organized capitalism by a "class compromise" that allows economic crises to be mitigated and class consciousness to be fragmented. Whereas in liberal capitalism the state seeks simply to secure the conditions for capitalists to make a profit, in organized capitalism the state pursues a conscious strategy of "crisis avoidance" and actually replaces the market in a number of areas. These actions smooth out the business cycle and mitigate the harmful side effects of the market.

Crisis Tendencies in Organized Capitalism

Habermas sees the problems of organized capitalism as being similar to those experienced by traditional societies when their principle of organization is called into question by the need to increase production. In organized capitalism, the state's intervention in the economy places the political system under contradictory imperatives (p. 62). The political system must prop up a production process that automatically makes the owners of corporations wealthier and the workers poorer, yet the state is expected to serve the interests of the entire population. In Habermas's words:

> The state apparatus is faced with two tasks. On the one hand, it is supposed to raise the requisite amount of taxes by skimming off profits and income and to use the available taxes so rationally that crisis-ridden disturbances of growth can be avoided. On the other hand, the selective raising of taxes, the discernable pattern of priorities in their use, and the administrative performances themselves must be so constituted that the need for legitimation can be satisfied as it arises.

Habermas sees economic and legitimation problems occurring more or less simultaneously as the state seeks to steer a course between them. The state is unable to correct all of the economy's defects because it is prohibited by the society's ideology from violating the boundary between the government and the economy. The state must manipulate the private decisions of individual capitalists, consumers, and workers with monetary incentives, and yet the more production is socialized, the less effective these incentives are. Furthermore, as the state becomes involved in previously unadministered areas of life in order to maintain the economy, the public begins to hold it responsible for economic and social conditions. Thus, while its ability to steer the economy is declining, public expectations are rising. It is for this reason, Habermas says, that the state in capitalist societies is constantly failing to achieve goals *"that it has placed on itself"* (p. 69).

Habermas believes that the state can avoid these problems only if it can somehow avoid having to show, on a case-by-case basis, that its administrative actions actually serve the interests of everyone rather than the special interests of capitalists. In his view, the state is already trying to take this path as it attempts to retreat "into a pretended sphere of objective forces in which political questions are interpreted as technical questions and specialists are immunized against the latent or suppressed dissent of those affected" (p. 134). Presupposing that capitalism is the best possible way to satisfy generalizable interests, the state defines public problems as problems of system maintenance and presents its policies as technically correct solutions to them, using the authority of science to support its claim. Habermas refers to this new ideology as a "technocratic consciousness," and he would include in it the cognitive-instrumental conception of rationality that we have discussed.

Nevertheless, Habermas says, even if the state is successful in suppressing political questions, a "motivation crisis" will result as people lose their belief that what they are doing is right and serves a purpose. In Habermas's view, motives are formed through communicative processes where people explore the arguments behind social norms and decide for themselves what to value and believe. If this questioning is blocked, people have emotional difficulties that take the form of social disorder, random crime, mental illness, alcoholism, and so on (anomie), as well as a general rejection of the system (alienation). Habermas leaves open the question of whether the disaffected can be mobilized for political action.

Altogether, then, Habermas says that organized capitalist societies experience "a bundle of crisis tendencies that, from a genetic point of view, represent a hierarchy of crisis phenomena shifted upwards from below" (p. 93). The system's economic crisis tendencies are processed and softened by the state, but the state encounters a rationality deficit because its activities weaken the effectiveness of exchange as a steering mechanism. Moreover, as the state intervenes in the economy and the educational system, it generates increased needs for legitimation because it makes areas of life contingent that were previously viewed as given. Expected to justify more and more activities when in fact both the complexity of the system and the imperatives of the economy make justification difficult, the state experiences legitimation crises. Finally, the state can deal with legitimation deficits by immunizing itself from the public with a technocratic ideology that suppresses practical questions from politics, but, says Habermas, this leads to motivation crises in the form of anomie and alienation. All of these crisis tendencies—economic, rationality, legitimation, and motivation—work together and are interchangeable, thus providing the state with a limited planning capacity, which can be used for purposes of "reactive crisis avoidance."

Habermas's Ideal

Habermas says that the interest behind his examination of crisis tendencies in advanced capitalism "is in exploring the possibilities of a 'post-modern' society" (p. 17). He says that in postmodern society, "substantive democracy" would replace the "formal democracy" now found in capitalist societies. Formal democracy is "a legitimation process that elicits generalized motives—that is, diffuse mass loyalty—but avoids participation" (p. 36). Because in capitalist societies social priorities are set by private investment decisions, politics in these societies is democratic in form only. Regardless of which political party holds office, the administrative system is committed to the same task, namely, administering the economy so that crises are avoided. In contrast, Habermas says,

Investment

substantive democracy would provide for "genuine participation of citizens in processes of political will-formation" (p. 36).

In effect, substantive democracy would institutionalize the norms that Habermas claims are presupposed by ordinary language. "In taking up practical discourse," he says, "we unavoidably suppose an ideal speech situation that, on the strength of its formal properties, allows consensus only through generalizable interests" (p. 110). When people enter an argument about how they should live, they assume, although usually counterfactually, that (1) the validity claims on which recommendations, warnings, norms, and the like are based are the exclusive object of discussion; (2) participants, themes, and contributions are not restricted; (3) no force except that of the better argument is exercised; and (4) all motives except that of the cooperative search for the truth are excluded. Habermas says these are "fundamental norms of rational speech that we must always presuppose if we discourse at all" (p. 110). For Habermas, substantive democracy would actualize the conditions necessary for these norms to be realized.

Habermas warns, however, against equating substantive democracy with any particular form of organization. For one thing, the technology that makes communication possible on a mass scale changes. Consequently, the extent to which collective "will formation" can be democratized is not fixed. For another thing, the amount of coerciveness needed by the state cannot be assumed to remain constant, since, as Habermas notes, "no one can know (today) the degree to which aggressiveness can be curtailed and the voluntary recognition of discursive principles attained" (p. 36). Third, the scope of public decisions should be open to expansion or contraction. In any social system there will be spheres of action in which individuals pursue their own interests, but the particular activities that are to be left unregulated should remain a political question. In short, Habermas suggests that in substantive democracy the organization of political participation would itself be subject to ongoing public consideration.

As Habermas sees it, substantive democracy would allow

practical reason to guide the development of technical knowledge, that is, allow generalizable interests to steer the economy (*Toward a Rational Society*, pp. 62–80). From Habermas's perspective, the problems that capitalist societies are unable to solve follow from a principle of organization that removes investment decisions from political consideration and thus allows technical innovation to proceed in an uncontrolled, "nature-like" fashion. Although under organized capitalism the state is now actively involved in organizing science for the production of new technologies, these technologies are either exploited secretly for military purposes, or else they enter a commercial economy and serve "preexisting, unreflected social interests." Consequently, technological development occurs behind the public's back and gives the appearance of being an objective force that no one can control, thus substantiating the technocratic consciousness of elites who see their task as one of adapting people to a changing technology. In contrast, Habermas argues, substantive democracy would allow a long-range research policy to be established on the basis of generalizable interests ascertained through public discussion.

Criticisms and Rejoinders

Habermas has been criticized from two different perspectives, but in both cases the thesis is that his theory fails to provide a clear set of political principles. Those working out of a traditional Marxist framework have been troubled that Habermas fails to identify a revolutionary subject to fill the role played in Marxism by the proletariat, and, further, that he does not present any specific institutional forms to replace liberal democracy (see Bernstein, 1976; McCarthy, 1978, p. 385). On the other hand, authors who are sympathetic to traditional liberalism believe that Habermas has paid inadequate attention to the recognized potential of modern states to become totalitarian (Hill, 1972; Heather and Stolz, 1979). In their view, Habermas's philosophy leaves open the possibility of unchecked political power because it does not defend individual rights.

Admittedly, these criticisms are not groundless. As we have already seen, Habermas steadfastly refuses to provide an institutional design for substantive democracy, and a review of his lifetime works shows that he has spent much more time on epistemological issues than on politics. However this does not mean that his theory is devoid of clear political implications.

White (1980) has drawn two political principles from Habermas's theory of communicative action. In his words (p. 1015):

First, there is the freedom to participate in public decisions important to one's basic concerns; and, second, freedom of expression and tolerance. These procedural political principles state minimal conditions for a politics that claims democratic legitimacy.

The principles are inherent in the ideal speech situation that Habermas says is presupposed by language.

Of the two principles, the requirement of participation has radical implications, because, unlike tolerance and free expression, it has not yet been adopted by any modern society. It would mean, for example, establishing mechanisms for two-way communication in politics (see *Theory of Communicative Action,* pp. 371–72); making employer relocation decisions publicly accountable; and democratizing areas of life, such as school and work, that are now administered bureaucratically because they are currently viewed as outside the public sphere.

Of course, this raises the questions of how these institutional changes are going to be kept from degenerating into majority tyranny or totalitarianism, and what social groups or classes are going to carry them out. With respect to the latter issue, Habermas points to the new social movements of feminism, environmentalism, and peace as the carriers of a new philosophy that demands democracy in a number of new areas (family, work) and interjects new considerations into the political process (natural resources, quality of life, future generations). These groups are not like Marx's proletariat; they do not comprise the bulk of the population, and they are not driven by economic forces to come to their political positions. But from Habermas's perspectives they are the carriers of a new political and ethical philosophy that, because it is grounded in the fundamental norms of communication, has the potential to bring the prevailing ideology into question.

As to whether the principle of participation will lead to totalitarianism, Habermas's theory implies, to the contrary, that public expectations will increasingly limit the conditions under which authority can be exercised. Indeed, this narrowing of authority can already be seen. In just the past fifty years, the rights of employees, children, students, women, the handicapped, and many other groups have expanded dramatically, even though their newly won rights extend beyond the public sphere. Habermas's theory traces this cultural development to people's built-in expectation that norms must be discursively justified, and it implies that this force will also hold democratic procedures within acceptable bounds.

Culture
Norms of Rationality
Science
("translation")

Norms of Discourse
Dialogue
Communication

Norms of Society
Politics / Ethics
Government

("negotiation")

Chapter 7
Cultural and Psychological Impacts of Suppressed Issues

HABERMAS'S THEORY draws our attention to the possibility that the Great Society was a collective self-deception that transformed class conflicts into psychic conflicts. The most important question from his perspective is whether the policy framework recognized and directly addressed the conflicting interests of capital and labor. This question redirects our focus to yet another domain of inquiry. We began, with the cultural theory of poverty and the theory of welfare dependency, by examining the immediate impacts of the Great Society on the poverty population, particularly with regard to the source of the poverty culture and the effects of economic growth on the incomes of the poor. Next, Lindblom's theory led us to focus on the relationship between politico-economic mechanisms and public opinion. We saw from this perspective that the Great Society had its most profound impacts where it altered business privileges. In this, our fourth cut at the Great Society, Habermas asks us to look not at the policy framework and its intended effects but at what policy makers said and did and how their claims and actions affected the system's legitimacy.

Habermas's Explanation of Poverty

A sketch of Habermas's conception of organized capitalism is presented in figure 7-1. The triangular placement of subsystems, with the sociocultural system at the top and the economic system at the bottom, is designed to capture the image of "crisis tendencies displaced upward from below." Habermas's thesis is that public policies in advanced capitalism alter the capitalist principle of organization and threaten to repoliticize class relations, which under liberal capitalism are regulated entirely by the automatic functioning of labor markets. In theory, economic crises force the state to protect workers from the uncontrollable side effects of the market, but the state's responsibility for the condition of workers must be constantly renounced and denied to avoid having class struggles break out in politics. The result of this syndrome of denial and hesitation is, supposedly, a series of economic, rationality, legitimation, and motivation crises.

In using this analysis to develop an explanation of poverty, we would naturally begin in the economic system. Drawing on the work of O'Connor (1978), Habermas argues that state intervention in the economy has divided the economy into separate public, monopoly, and competitive sectors. Jobs in the public and monopoly sectors, which are the main beneficiaries of the political system's steering activities, have relatively high wages because labor in these sectors is organized and wages are set politically through negotiation. In contrast, jobs in the competitive sector often leave workers in poverty because they are characterized by high turnover, low pay, and limited opportunity for advancement. By implication, the relative size of the three sectors determines the amount of poverty existing at any given time. Although policies designed to equalize wages across the three sectors or to shrink the size of the competitive sector would reduce poverty, such policies are blocked by labor and management in the monopolistic and public sectors, both of which benefit from a large competitive sector.[1]

Habermas's thesis that the sociocultural system has an inherent logic that can see through biased policies requires that he explain the failure of lower classes in organized capitalism to rebel against this situation. He cannot conclude, as Lindblom does, that demands for equality are simply excluded from consideration in politics, for he assumes that people have minds of their own and hence that public opinion is independent of elite discourse. Moreover, Habermas is quite clear that the basic thrust of policy in organized capitalism is fundamentally unfair. Taxes are raised from everyone, but they are spent largely on armaments, space travel, and infrastructure

Figure 7-1. Habermas's Conception of Organized Capitalism

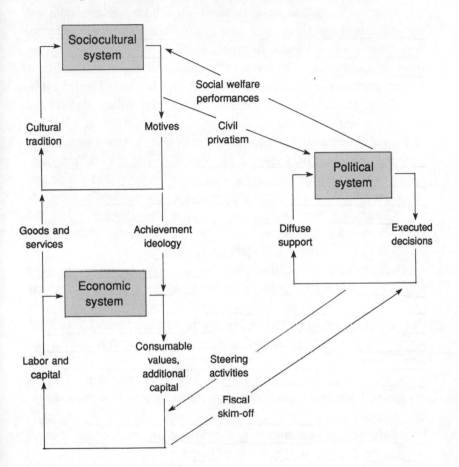

that benefit the large capital-intensive industries and their workers. Public policy is thus characterized by "the contradiction of socialized production for nongeneralizable goals" (p. 39). Why do workers in the competitive sector not see this and demand a change?

Habermas's explanation is twofold. First, he argues that political leaders control the public with propaganda, the authority of science, "symbolic politics," and other methods for separating legitimation from administration. Contrary to Lindblom's claim that political leaders remain silent on primary issues and have no further problems from the citizenry, Habermas argues that policy makers are constantly walking a thin line between an achievement ideology and popular demands for income redistribution. On the one hand, to suppress class conflicts they must appeal to the notion that capitalism is an equitable system for allocating income, and yet on the other hand they must redistribute income to correct obvious inequities. Concealing this contradiction requires considerable effort and skill. Thus what Lindblom calls "circularity" is for Habermas a carefully orchestrated and precarious deception.

Second, Habermas claims that the educational system has been adjusted to assist the political system in keeping class conflicts latent. "The educational processes lead to motivational structures that are class specific, that is, to the repressive authority of conscience and an individualistic achievement orientation among the bourgeoisie, and to external superego structures and a conventional work morality in the lower class" (p. 77). The separation of legitimation and administration in formal democracy has its psychological corollary in the separation of conscience and will in personalities. Relations of domination and privilege are anchored in a rigid conscience that is inaccessible to criticism.[2]

Thus, for Habermas the peculiar attitudes and limited abilities of the lower class are not, as the culture of poverty theory suggests, the result of isolation from mainstream institutions; nor do they stem from the dominance of single males in poor communities; nor, indeed, are they the result of the sort of class indoctrination that Lindblom has in mind, wherein the poor simply have a limited imagination because of constraints on elite discourse. To the contrary, for Habermas the "uncoerced obedience, fatalism, and orientation to immediate gratification" (p. 77) of the lower class is a character deformation created through the educational system to counter natural tendencies that would raise questions about inequality in capitalism. Freethinking must be and often is expunged, even though in some cases the end product is a human being who is scarcely human.

Of course, consistent with his sociocultural premise, Habermas believes that the political system's efforts to maintain its legitimacy exact a psychological toll among the poor and the nonpoor alike. The price paid is motivation problems, particularly among adolescents and young adults. In Habermas's view, socialization is neither smooth nor guaranteed. Each new generation must be convinced that the system's legitimating ideology is true. To the extent that discursive redemption of the system's worldview is blocked by a politics that fails to address class conflicts directly, many young people will either rebel or withdraw.

Analysis of the Great Society

In looking at the Great Society, Habermas's theory allows us to see something that until now we have failed to notice: The evolution of the Great Society was inconsistent with its initial legitimation.

An Unconscious Shift in Policy

Ostensibly, the Great Society was designed not to supplant the functioning of labor markets but rather to improve their efficiency by enhancing the employability of workers and prohibiting racial, ethnic, and religious discrimination. The rhetoric surrounding the policy framework claimed that the poor were to be given "a hand, not a hand-out." In actuality, though, the Great Society was largely a welfare program. Table 7-1 lists federal expenditures as percentages of total budget outlays for social action programs, in-kind transfers, and cash transfers. Initially, policy makers lived up to their promises. Between 1963 and 1967, the percentage of the

budget going to income transfers declined, while the percentage going to social action and in-kind transfers expanded. After 1967,
however, the direction of growth changed. Expenditures for social
action leveled off, expenditures for in-kind transfers grew moder-
ately, and income transfers skyrocketed. By 1975, transfer programs
accounted for half of the federal budget, whereas less than 5 percent
of the budget was devoted to the social programs that were supposed to be the core of the Great Society. The claim that the Great
Society primarily enhanced the qualifications of workers is patently
false.

Table 7-1. Federal Expenditures on Human Resources,
by Categories, as a Percentage of Total
Budget Outlays, 1963–75

	1963 (%)	1967 (%)	1971 (%)	1975 (%)
Social action	1.09	3.56	4.60	4.66
In-kind transfers	3.08	6.01	8.83	11.18
Income transfers	30.23	26.57	35.17	38.81

Source: Extracted from table 1-A3, Henry J. Aaron, *Politics and the Professors: The Great Society in Perspective* (Washington: The Brookings Institution, 1978).

The expansion of income transfers after 1967 was accomplished
through changes in a number of programs. Some of the most important ones were large increases and broader coverage for retirement
benefits under the Social Security Act; a doubling (from 26 weeks
to 52 weeks) of the length of time payments were made under
unemployment insurance; liberalization of federal workers' compensation programs, veterans' benefits, and public assistance for the
aged and blind; and expanded coverage under Aid to Families with
Dependent Children (AFDC) (for a detailed analysis, see Lynn,
1977). On top of the expansion of income transfers came two in-
kind benefits—food stamps and medical care—that were intro-

duced in 1964 and 1965 and became huge programs by the mid-1970s.

The expansion of the welfare system was not focused exclusively or even primarily on the truly destitute. To be sure, much of the increase in income transfers went to the elderly, who could not have been expected to earn their way out of poverty like the other poor people targeted by the Great Society, but this was only part of the story. In the late 1960s a fundamental change occurred in the nation's welfare programs: Increasingly, they began to serve people who had other sources of income. This shift was especially pronounced in AFDC. Prior to 1967, AFDC payments were reduced dollar for dollar against earned income; after 1967, beneficiaries could keep the first $30 of earnings plus one-third of their additional earnings without any offsetting reductions in AFDC payments. Almost overnight, welfare was transformed into a system that supplanted, or at least modified, the traditional allocation of income through labor markets.[3]

The shift in the Great Society from social action to income transfers, and the change in income transfers from welfare to an earnings supplement, were not accompanied by a change in philosophy. Indeed, the reverse is true.[4] While policy makers were turning the Great Society into exactly what in 1964 they had said they opposed, they repeatedly appealed to the public's achievement orientation. AFDC's "thirty dollars and one-third rule" was packaged as a change to promote labor force entry. Extensions in the duration of payments under Unemployment Insurance were presented as an "economic stimulus." The provision of food stamps to families with incomes above the poverty line was introduced as an attack on "poverty-related hunger." In each instance, the welfare expansion included a work incentive of some sort, but the incentive was largely symbolic.[5] Thus the change in the Great Society was made unconsciously. In the words of Charles Murray (p. 45):

Before 1964, we did not debate welfare for working people because the reasons against it were so self-evident; after 1967 we did not debate the issue because the reasons in favor of it were so self-evident. There was no great debate in the interim, no moment at which the nation could observe itself changing its national policy. The change happened unannounced.

Social Action

Habermas's theory leads us to look for these same contradictions between symbolism and substance in social action programs. During the unconscious transformation of the Great Society as a whole, the social action core of the policy framework was redirected as well. The evolution of occupational skills training, compensatory education, and community action mirrored in microcosm the shift in the Great Society from its original objective of qualifying the labor force to its ultimate emphasis on income maintenance. In short order, social action became a disguised expansion of the public sector.

At the start of the Great Society, what were then called "manpower programs" had the objective of improving the skills of the unemployed. However, in the early 1970s the objective shifted to "job creation." (For an excellent study of employment and training policy during this period, see Baumer and Van Horn, 1985.) Expenditures for *training* under the Comprehensive Employment and Training Act (CETA), which was passed in 1973 to consolidate the nation's programs in this area, averaged around $2 billion annually. In contrast, public service employment programs, always proposed as temporary measures to reduce unemployment, were the tail that wagged the CETA dog. Spending on "jobs programs" averaged around $4 billion each year during the decade.[6] Between 1977 and 1979, they ran at $13 billion annually (Baumer and Van Horn, 1985, p. 18). In general, the public service employment jobs were in state, city, and county governments, particularly in public works, transportation, parks and recreation, and social services (Mirengoff and Rindler, 1978, p. 166). Less than half the workers in public service employment had incomes below the poverty level before coming onto the government payroll (Baumer and Van Horn, 1985, table 3-2, p. 79).

A similar phenomenon characterized compensatory education. As previously stated, the failure of Head Start to produce lasting improvements in the learning achievements of preschoolers led policy makers to work on the public elementary schools. However, rather than tacking on programs, they simply allocated federal monies to the nation's school districts on the basis of the number of economically disadvantaged students in each district. At the local level, the monies were seldom concentrated on the students in poverty, and sometimes they were spent on frivolous items like football jerseys and swimming pools (Murphy, 1971; Levin, 1977, p. 134). In the end, compensatory education turned into revenue sharing for the public schools.

Finally, the Community Action Program (CAP) also appears to have been something other than what its rationale implied. The strategy of implementing federal programs through Community Action Agencies may have been initiated as an effort to organize the poor for political participation, and the strategy may have been subverted after the Model Cities Program. But from the perspective provided by Habermas the most significant aspect of CAP is that, in effect, it created a new sector of the economy, neither wholly public nor entirely private. In the words of Kenneth Boulding (1973), CAP evolved into a "grants economy" along side the "exchange economy." The grants economy is composed primarily of private, not-for-profit corporations that obtain government grants to provide social services. Salamon (1984, pp. 263–64) estimates that today there are approximately 375,000 service-providing, nonprofit corporations, and that together they spend $114 billion annually and employ 4.6 million people.[7] A large majority of these corporations were formed after 1960.

Thus, when we look once more at social action programs, this time through a Habermasian lens, we see that the programs did not so much enhance the abilities of the poor as restructure the economy. The majority of monies for employment and training went to create jobs in the public sector. Compensatory education was actually compensatory funding for the nation's school districts. And community action created, or at least drastically expanded, the grants economy. From this perspective, the efforts of policy analysts to identify the effects of job training on employment and earnings, compensatory education on learning achievement, and community action on political organization missed what was really happening in public policy during the Great Society.

Explaining the Transformation

Although Habermas would argue that the contradiction between the Great Society's legitimation and its evolution in practice is evidence of the conflicting pressures placed on the political system by economic and sociocultural imperatives, other interpretations could be offered for the direction that policy took in the late 1960s and early '70s. For example, Murray says that the shift toward welfare and away from social action was caused by a change of "fashion" among "the intelligentsia" (p. 42). In his view the "elite wisdom" changed, but the change was never debated in mass politics. Still another perspective, common in political science, is that the politics of legitimation differs from that of legislation and administration. This perspective suggests that in electoral politics the public chose "a hand and not a handout" but once policy making entered Congress and the bureaucracy, organized interests took control and redirected the Great Society toward cash benefits.

Habermas's analysis depends on three related theorems: (1) poverty could not have been reduced by enhancing the qualifications of workers; (2) the expansion of government activity in the labor market caused class conflicts to break out in politics and hence had to be concealed; and (3) the effort to conceal the Great Society's new direction caused legitimation problems.

Poverty in Organized Capitalism. Habermas's conception of organized capitalism implies that social action, in the absence of income transfers or some other approach for improving the wages of workers, could not reduce the incidence of poverty in America. In theory, the heart of the problem of poverty resides in the division of the economy into a competitive sector on the one hand and monopoly and public sectors on the other. Habermas argues that, as mechanization is stimulated in the monopoly sector by public policies that produce new technologies, employment in the monopoly sector declines faster than it rises in the public sector. The result is that a larger and larger proportion of the labor force is employed in the competitive sector where wages are set through the market, and the incidence of poverty necessarily increases. Policies that prop up the monopoly sector, even though they benefit big business and organized labor, lead to lower wages and to higher rates of poverty and unemployment. Mechanization and poverty go hand in hand.

Evidence in support of Habermas's three-sector model of the economy is available from the U.S. Bureau of the Census. During the Great Society, total employment almost doubled, but the increase was concentrated in the least lucrative economic sector, the competitive sector. Table 7-2 shows the distribution of the employed population by sector for 1962 and 1980. (The table was constructed by collapsing the typology of industrial sectors used by the Census Bureau. The various industries included in the competitive, monopoly, and public sectors are listed at the bottom of the table.) Between 1962 and 1980, the monopoly and public sectors

Table 7-2: Sector of the Employed Population, 1962 and 1980

	Percent		Number (in 1000s)	
	1962	1980	1962	1980
Monopoly and public sectors[a]	46	42	31,770	48,194
Competitive sector[b]	54	58	28,276	53,038
Total	100	100	60,046	101,232

Source: U.S. Bureau of the Census, *Statistical Abstract of the United States,* 1963 (table 291, p. 220; table 310, p. 236) and 1985 (table 679, p. 416).

a. Includes manufacturing; transportation, communication, and other public utilities; finance, insurance, real estate; and public administration.

b. Includes agriculture, forestry, and fisheries; mining; construction; wholesale trade; retail trade; and service industries.

expanded by about 17 million workers while the competitive sector grew by almost 25 million. This expansion of the competitive sector would have been expected to have caused an increase in the number of families in poverty, but it was offset by (1) an increase in income transfers and (2) the entry of females into the labor market and the corresponding rise in two-worker families. The percentage of households in poverty thus declined, but the distribution of poverty was shifted toward the young and toward one-worker families. Those individuals who were not assisted by direct income transfers, or who for one reason on another did not adapt to labor market conditions by forming an economic partnership around marriage, were left without adequate incomes.

The redistribution of poverty from whites to blacks can also be explained from the same premises. Table 7-3 (page 112) shows the sector of the employed population in 1962 and 1980 for whites and nonwhites. The improved earnings of nonwhites relative to whites is attributable, at least in part, to a racial shift in employment by sector. Between 1962 and 1980, nonwhite employment in the monopoly and public sectors expanded from 30 percent of the nonwhite labor force to 43 percent, while white employment declined from 43 percent to 40 percent. By the end of the 1970s, whites were less likely on average than nonwhites to be in industries with the best wages.

Thus, there is support for the thesis that poverty could not have been reduced by programs to enhance the skills and abilities of the poor. If the economy is divided into sectors, and if training is limited to the competitive sector, then training and other efforts to improve the qualifications of workers could not have reduced poverty. In fact, such programs may have contributed to the problem of poverty by facilitating the expansion of the competitive sector.[8]

Class Conflicts. Up to this point, we have not considered the context of social disorder that surrounded the Great Society, but Habermas's arguments about the constant threat of class conflicts in organized capitalism lead us now to look at this aspect of the 1960s. Although the transformation of the Great Society into a massive welfare program occurred without an explicit legitimation, it was

Table 7-3: Sector of the Employed Population,
1962 and 1980, by Race

	Nonwhite		White	
	1962 (%)	1980 (%)	1962 (%)	1980 (%)
Monopoly and public sectors[a]	30	43	43	40
Competitive sector[b]	70	57	57	60

Source: Adapted from tables 12.1 and 12.2 in Lou Ferleger, "Explaining away Black Poverty: The Structural Determinants of Black Unemployment," in *Applied Poverty Research,* edited by Richard Goldstein and Stephen M. Sachs, pp. 148–74 (Totowa, NJ: Rowman and Allanheld, 1984).
a. Includes manufacturing; transportation, communication, and other public utilities; finance, insurance, real estate; and public administration.
b. Includes agriculture, forestry, and fisheries; mining; construction; wholesale trade; retail trade; and service industries.

preceded and accompanied by violence of frightening proportions. When historians look back on this period, they will probably consider the black riots of the 1960s to have been the most important events of the decade.

Habermas's theory implies that the Great Society was at least partly responsible for sparking the disorder, and there is evidence to support this hypothesis. Prior to 1964, the civil rights movement was overwhelmingly nonviolent. In the incidents of violence that did occur, blacks were victims rather than perpetrators. If the civil rights movement had a single beginning, it was the bus boycott in Montgomery, Alabama, in 1956. If the nonviolent thrust of the movement had a clear end, it was the so-called long hot summer of 1964. From 1964 through 1972, urban riots occurred every year.

Although antipoverty workers and program participants were not directly responsible for the urban disorder of the 1960s, they were actively involved in much of the social agitation of the period. A brief chronology of events, just for 1966, makes this clear. (The following is drawn from Sobel, 1977.)

January 24: Twenty-two blacks staged a sit-in at the Economic Opportunity Committee's New York office to demand more jobs for Harlem's blacks.

January 31: Organized by the Poor People's Conference, about 50 impoverished black Mississippians invaded the deactivated Greenville Air Force Base demanding food, housing, and jobs.

February 11: Forty-eight black five-year-olds from Mississippi, accompanied by 25 adults, invaded the hearing room of the U.S. House Education and Labor Committee demanding that their application for a Head Start grant be expedited.

March 31: Ninety unemployed black plantation workers from Mississippi set up tents in Washington. D.C., in a protest against delays in their applications for antipoverty funds. The demonstrators represented three local community organizations.

June 30: One thousand demonstrators, organized by the Ohio Steering Committee for Adequate Welfare, marched to the Ohio state capitol building to demand an increase in welfare payments.

August 23: Antipoverty workers in Jersey City, New Jersey, staged sit-ins at the Office of Economic Opportunity's New York City office to demand greater control over the city's antipoverty programs.

September 27: Five hundred demonstrators participated in a Poor People's March on Washington "to protest the current lack of concern for effective antipoverty legislation."

In 1967, the National Organization for Welfare Rights was formed and held its first convention; in just a few years it had 125,000 members located in over 180 cities and in all 50 states. In 1968, Dr. Martin Luther King led a Poor People's March on Washington, D.C.

The chronology could go on. The important point is that, in just a few years, the civil rights movement had become a class movement, a "poor people's movement" demanding jobs, food, welfare, and power.

Legitimation Deficits. As we have seen, the political system's

response to this situation was to play it both ways—to stick to the
rhetoric of "a hand, not a handout," but at the same time to expand
the system of in-kind and income transfers. As Habermas's theory
would have led us to predict, this duplicity had its costs, albeit less
for the politicians than for the system as a whole. The decline in the
public's confidence in prevailing institutions has been well documented. Table 7-4 lists the percentage of respondents in national

Table 7-4. Assessment of Key Institutions

	Percentages of the public stating that they have "a great deal of confidence" in certain institutions		
	1976 (%)	1971 (%)	1966 (%)
Medicine	42	61	73
Higher education	31	37	61
Television news	28	—	—
Organized religion	24	27	41
The military	23	27	62
The U.S. Supreme Court	22	23	50
The press	20	18	29
Major companies	16	27	55
Executive branch of the federal government	11	23	41
Organized labor	10	14	22
Congress	9	19	42

"legitimacy crisis" [handwritten annotation]

Source: Everett Carll Ladd, Jr., "The Polls: The Question of Confidence,"
Public Opinion Quarterly (Winter, 1976–77): 544–52. Ladd's data are taken
from *The Harris Survey*, 22 March 1976; and *The Harris Survey Yearbook of
Public Opinion*, 1971, p. 60.

polls stating that they have "a great deal of confidence" in certain
institutions. Most of the percentages were fairly large beginning in
1966, but they all declined precipitously in later years. By 1976,
every institution was resting at its all-time low.

Of course, we have no way of knowing whether the observed

decline in confidence was due to the Great Society or to such other factors as Vietnam and Watergate. However, it is significant that polls show low confidence for most of the institutions through the end of the '70s and into the '80s.[9] If widespread skepticism about the nation's institutions were due to the personalities of office-holders or to particular decisions, then a change in leadership together with a reversal of policy should have altered the public's opinion. That the lack of confidence remains suggests that legitimation problems are deep and serious.

Overall, the picture that emerges is of a political system working at cross-purposes. Responding to a nonviolent civil rights movement, policy makers established the beginnings of the Great Society in 1964 and 1965. Initially consistent with an achievement ideology, it focused on social action programs designed to enhance the skills and abilities of the poor. In turn, black riots erupted in the cities, and the civil rights movement became a class movement demanding money, employment, and power. The polity reacted by expanding the welfare system and transforming social action programs into a quasi-public appendage of the economic system, all the while presenting these programmatic expansions and shifts in the guise of welfare reform, "temporary" jobs creation, and "economic stimulus." The riots ended, but the public turned cynical about the society's institutions. Thus, in dealing with class conflicts, the political system undermined its own legitimacy.

Challenges to Habermas

While Habermas's theory can thus account for many of the results of the Great Society, it is challenged by the direction taken under the Reagan Revolution. Fundamentally, Habermas's theory rests on the assumption that people are creatures who must be convinced of the correctness of laws, rules, and norms. Unlike Lindblom, who sees "circularity" as a stable phenomenon, Habermas begins from the premise that false legitimations can be, and indeed are, inevitably seen through. His theory of history is, at bottom, a theory of how and when the ideological spells of exploitative social systems are broken and replaced.

When Habermas wrote *Legitimation Crisis,* his thesis appeared quite tenable. The Western industrial democracies were experiencing widespread urban unrest and organized social movements from women, blacks, students, and other groups. In particular, the student movement seemed to validate Habermas's argument that the greatest threat to the establishment is the academic community. Habermas believed that the social sciences were being used politically to screen out the demands of the disadvantaged. Clearly, students raised this issue when they demanded that courses be "relevant," that research for the defense sector be moved off campus, and that universities withdraw their investments from companies with holdings in South Africa and other "exploitative" countries. Similarly, the decline of the public's trust in government also supported Habermas's view that the state was slowly but surely losing its legitimacy. In the 1960s and early 1970s, journalists spoke often of the "credibility gap," and a legitimation crisis appeared imminent if not already in progress.

Today, though, Habermas's theory seems less convincing. The Reagan administration succeeded in withdrawing the government from areas of the economy that were previously heavily administered. The civil rights movement is subdued, the women's movement is changing its direction, university campuses are reporting a new student conservatism, and the radical generation of the 1960s is the yuppie population of today, a group noted for its materialism and privatism. Certainly, it can be argued that Habermas's claims about the intractable position of the political system are incorrect, and that, to the contrary, policy makers satisfied the public simply by enhancing equality of opportunity. How might Habermas account for the system's apparent ability to restabilize itself?

The rejoinder implied by his theory is that the legitimation problems of the 1960s and '70s have been replaced by the motivation problems of the '80s. Table 7-5 shows the suicide rates of different age groups for 1970 and 1980. (Data by age for 1960 are not avail-

Table 7-5. Suicides per 100,000 Population, by Age,
1970 and 1980

Age	1970	1980
Less than 5	1	2
5 to 9	7	8
15 to 19	6	8
20 to 24	13	16
25 to 29	15	17
30 to 34	15	15
35 to 44	18	15
45 to 54	21	16
55 to 64	22	16
65 and over	22	18

Sources: Population data from U.S. Bureau of the Census, *Census of Population: 1970*, vol. 1, Washington, 1973, pp. 1–572; and *Census of Population: 1980*, vol. 1, Washington, 1983, pp. 1–67. Suicide data from National Center for Health Statistics, *Vital Statistics of the United States, 1980*, vol. 2, Mortality, Part A (DHHS Pub. No. PHS 85-1101), Public Health Service, Washington, 1985, p. 297; and *Vital Statistics of the United States, 1970*, vol. 2, Mortality, Part A (HRA 75-1101), Public Health Service, Washington, 1985, pp. 1–184.

able.) Although the changes in suicide rates are not particularly large in either direction, their association with age conforms with Habermas's theory. Suicide has increased among all the age groups under thirty years old, and it has decreased for all the groups over thirty-five.

Drug abuse shows a similar pattern. Table 7-6 lists the lifetime prevalence trends for the use of strong drugs by youths, young adults, and older adults. The numbers in the table are the percentages of each group who at any time in their lives had used hallucinogens, inhalants, cocaine, heroin, or other opiates. The increase in the use of strong drugs is quite large among youths and young adults. In 1962, less than one-half of one percent of the nation's youths had used "hard" drugs; by 1972, the percentage was up to 8. Similarly, only 3 percent of young adults had used drugs in 1962, but one-third had used them by 1979.

Table 7-6. Stronger Drugs:[a] Lifetime Prevalence Trends

	1962[b] (%)	1967[b] (%)	1972 (%)	1976 (%)	1979 (%)
Youth	<0.5	3	8	9	9
Young adult	3	4	17	25	33
Older adult	1	1	2	4	6

Sources: Cisin, I.; Miller, J.; and Harrell, A., *Highlights from the National Survey on Drug Abuse: 1977* (Washington, 1978), and Fishburne, P.; Abelson, H.; and Cisin, I., *The National Survey on Drug Abuse: Main Findings, 1979* (Washington, ????).
  a. Includes hallucinogens, inhalants, cocaine, heroin (except 1979), and other opiates: any one or any combination.
  b. Based on retrospective data collected in 1977.

As usual, we have no way of linking these increases back to the Great Society. No doubt many other explanations could be offered for the increase in suicide and drug abuse that has occurred among the nation's young people. The important point, though, is that Habermas's theory leads us to look in this direction. The argument that human beings must be given a convincing justification of the social order has highlighted a considerable amount of evidence from the Great Society, which otherwise we would have ignored.

Chapter 8
The Subject Matter of Policy Research

A PERSPECTIVAL ANALYSIS of the Great Society is at once both revealing and misleading. Although it is true that different theories lead to different interpretations of the facts, it is wrong to conclude from this that evidence can have no bearing on political disputes. Rather, the implication is that theoretical issues are unavoidable and hence need to be addressed head-on.

Policy Research Revisited

The prevailing approach to policy research has left us in an intellectual muddle precisely because it is insensitive to theoretical issues. When we look at all of the evidence considered in our analysis of the Great Society, we can see the limited utility of information about how well a given program achieves policy makers' objectives. Table 8-1 lists each explanation of poverty and the main findings supporting and challenging them.

The normal approach in policy analysis of focusing on client group impacts has two obvious problems. First, it ignores potentially crucial evidence about impacts outside the target population. The theories of Lindblom and Habermas, as well as those of the Reagan administration, directed our attention to impacts that the Great Society's designers would never have anticipated. These included rising unemployment and inflation, increases in racial tolerance, demands for equality of opportunity from minority groups other than blacks, legitimation problems, and urban unrest.

A second inadequacy of program performance data is that it can be interpreted in radically different ways depending on the theoretical context in which it is placed. Consider, for example, the

Table 8-1. Explanations of Poverty and Evidence
from the Great Society

Explanation	Supporting evidence	Challenging evidence
Cultural theory: Isolated workers develop low-achievement culture, which is resistant to change.	Initial reduction in incidence of poverty followed by leveling off; learning differences of the poor; temporariness of social action impacts.	Rapid changes in incidence of poverty across races; rapid increases in voting and income of blacks.
Supply-side: Income redistribution discourages investment and work; much poverty is voluntary.	Rising unemployment and inflation. Reduced labor force entry; increased family dissolution; temporariness of social action impacts.	Rapid changes in incidence of poverty across races; rapid increases in voting and income of blacks.
Lindblom: Markets maintain poverty. Private enterprise polyarchy gives business dominance and leads to suppression of primary issues.	Success of civil rights in redistributing poverty, reducing racism, and stimulating social movements; temporariness of social action impacts indicating indoctrination.	Reduced labor force entry from welfare.
Habermas: Markets maintain poverty. Principle of organization is in conflict with legitimations, causing contradictory policies and crises.	Inconsistency between Great Society's legitimation and its emphasis on transfers; shift in social action programs; temporariness of social action impacts; decline in public confidence.	End of social unrest; the new conservatism.

temporariness of the impacts from social action programs. This could mean that: (1) as the cultural theory of poverty suggests, poor communities have a culture caused by isolation, and this culture overcomes the effects of training, education, and community organization; or (2) following the theory of welfare dependency, the

poor have a culture dominated by single, separated, and divorced
males, and this culture not only overcomes the effects of social
action, it is intensified by income and in-kind transfers; or (3) as
Lindblom argues, the poor are indoctrinated by schools, the judicial
system, employers, and other mechanisms of socialization that
transmit the "business message"; or (4) as Habermas claims, sub-
mission to poverty is rooted in a rigid conscience, which makes
changes in motivation difficult to maintain. Clearly, something is
wrong when "the facts" have such little force in the argument.

In designing the methodology of policy research, policy analysts made a fundamental error. They assumed that the subject matter of policy research could be identified independent of a theoretical framework. This methodological assumption enabled policy
analysts to set as their goal the evaluation of "program performance." What it ignored is that neither programs nor performance
indicators are self-evident. To be sure, the difficulty of identifying
the goals of policy was recognized; a considerable amount of ink
was devoted in the literature to explaining how policy objectives
could be teased out of ambiguous and, in some instances, obviously
contradictory legislative directives. However, the possibility that
conflicting perspectives might conceptualize the subject matter of
policy analysis in entirely different ways was overlooked.

As we have seen, though, the essence of public policy is in the
eye of the beholder. From Lindblom's viewpoint, for example,
legislation is examined in terms of how it affects politico-economic
mechanisms, and impacts include not simply or even primarily
impacts on program participants but changes in the competition of
ideas. For Habermas, on the other hand, "public policy" is not only
what policy makers do about public problems but also what they
say and how their statements contradict their actions. In this case,
policy analysts look for evidence of legitimation and motivation
problems. Even when there is a recognizable program that everyone
agrees deserves attention, analysis is theory laden. Affirmative
action under civil rights laws can be treated as an alteration of the
balance between business and government that removes constraints
on volitions, or instead as a procedure for fragmenting class con-

sciousness and propping up an achievement ideology. The essential features of a given program lie hidden within the complexity of the social order. Depending on the viewpoint of the analyst, the same "program" would be broken into different components and evaluated against different indicators of performance. Without social and political theory, the subject matter of policy analysis has no clear structure and no obvious boundaries.

Significantly, the reverse of this conclusion is also true. Any approach to the evaluation of public policy entails substantive, theoretical commitments. We have seen that the narrow focus of most policy analysis rests on a cognitive-instrumental conception of rationality and on the related thesis that people's behavior is determined by their immediate circumstances. In trying to avoid theoretical issues by focusing on program performance, policy analysts have become unwitting partisans for the status quo.

Methodological Implications

The appropriate strategy for policy research is not to evaluate the extent to which a given program achieves policy makers' short-term objectives, but to design research so that, even if it is on a single program, it can help resolve the larger theoretical issues in politics. At least four kinds of research are needed: (1) analyses of policy formulation; (2) multi-theoretical assessments of target group impacts; (3) checks on auxiliary hypotheses; and (4) public opinion research on the relationship between public policy and mass politics.

Policy Formulation

Research is needed on policy formulation to track policy makers' theoretical premises and actions. Policy premises must be explicated so that it is possible to determine if policy makers' programs are consistent with their theoretical arguments. Otherwise, as our Habermasian analysis of the Great Society revealed, researchers risk overlooking unannounced policy shifts and directing their attention to program areas that have lost their centrality in the actual course of policy development.)

This approach to research on policy formulation differs from the two strategies currently common in political science. One political science approach is to examine policy development within narrowly defined programmatic areas. This focus is inappropriate for policy analysis because it ignores the larger theoretical context in which different program areas are situated. The most important policy shifts do not occur *within* policy areas but instead *across* them, as when, in the Great Society, income and in-kind transfers were vastly expanded while funding for social action programs grew little at all. Such shifts are visible only when the focus is on overall policy frameworks and the arguments used to justify them.

The second political science strategy used in investigating policy formulation is to focus on the overarching theories of different eras without following the details of program development. This approach tends to attribute too much rationality to the political process and can lead analysts to ignore major inconsistencies between policy makers' statements and their actions. If the Great Society is reconstructed from what policy makers said during the 1960s and '70s, one gets the mistaken impression that the policy framework was consistently developed to enhance labor market efficiency.

Target Group Impacts

Research on target group impacts should focus on domains of intervention where conflicting theories imply contradictory hypotheses. Crucial tests of this sort are not dissimilar to the kinds of program evaluations that policy analysts currently conduct, except that they entail a more complex conceptualization of possible impacts. The impacts that are to be measured must be developed on the basis of several theories, not just the theory underlying the program or advocated by policy makers.

Of particular importance are impacts involving the motivations of individuals and the subcultures of communities. As we have seen, the theories of Lindblom, Habermas, the Great Society, and the Reagan Revolution are in sharp disagreement over the role of culture in behavior. The Great Society posited a "culture of poverty" that is shortsighted and resistant to change. The Reagan Revolution assumed, in effect, that there is no culture; behavior follows economic incentives. Lindblom sees culture as malleable. In his view, class attitudes reflect the diffusion of information from a lopsided competition of ideas. Finally, Habermas conceptualizes culture as a collective identity that maintains the psychological integrity of individuals. These views imply contradictory hypotheses about the impacts from any number of programs.

Consider welfare. The expectation from the cultural theory of poverty is that welfare will have little effect on the motivations and social patterns of the poor. In this theory, the poor are already alienated and enculturated, and welfare will simply be absorbed into their existing life-style. The Reagan view, however, is that welfare breaks up families and leads to a culture dominated by the aspirations of single, shiftless males. From this perspective, an expansion of welfare should cause a chain reaction running from male-female relations to family composition and community role models. For his part, Lindblom would not be totally surprised by a reduction in work effort among the poor, but his theory points to additional impacts worthy of investigation, notably the interaction between labor market conditions and welfare's effects on work motives, and the possible influence of the humiliation associated with welfare on recipients' beliefs about the free market system. Habermas, of course, would look for signs of anomie. His hypothesis would be that welfare recipients will experience motivation problems because they lack control over their lives and yet are told that they could do well if only they were more diligent. The actual impacts of welfare, if examined from all these perspectives, could help analysts learn a great deal about motivation and the subculture of poor communities.

Many other programs could be examined in a similar way. The important point is to identify target group impacts with many different theories. No single crucial test will falsify a theory, but over

time a number of multi-theoretical projects might provide rea-
sonable grounds for believing one theory and doubting another.

Auxiliary Hypotheses

Auxiliary hypotheses present both a problem and an opportunity. They are problematic because they make it difficult, if not
impossible, to falsify a given theory. Nevertheless, investigating
such hypotheses can be the route to very important findings.

When we examined the Great Society from the perspectives offered by Lindblom and Habermas, we saw how this works. Lindblom's theory was challenged by the finding that welfare undermines work motives. On the face of it, the observation that welfare
reduced labor force entry raised doubts about Lindblom's claim that
income redistribution will not undermine work motives. However,
with the auxiliary hypothesis that meaningful work options can
overcome welfare's disincentives, we could reinterpret the findings
from guaranteed income experiments to mean that poor people
choose welfare over work because they have dismal employment
opportunities. When this reinterpretation was supported by Goodwin's research, it cast welfare's impacts on work incentives in an
entirely different light.

Similarly, Habermas's theory was called into question by the
recent turn to conservatism in American politics, but the theory provided a fallback position. The auxiliary hypothesis was that the
legitimation problems of the 1970s had been replaced by motivation problems in the 1980s. The rise of suicide and drug abuse
among youths and young adults supported this hypothesis and
made us wonder just how healthy the nation's newly found faith in
itself really is. Thus, a new fact can turn an existing fact inside out.

When defending their policies in the face of disappointing performance, policy makers frequently fall back on such auxiliary hypotheses. Proponents of the Great Society did not jettison their culture of poverty theory as the steady declines in poverty during the
1960s began to level off. Instead, they argued that the poverty culture was highly resistant to change and hence that it would take

more time and money to achieve the Great Society's objectives. Auxiliary hypotheses of this sort can and should be checked out.

Impacts on Politics and Public Opinion

Finally, it is most important to examine the effects of public policies on the very political processes that produce them (Lowi, 1973). The central question for policy research in the United States should be whether, and if so why, more government intervention in the economy means more, or less, freedom and democracy. This is the main issue dividing Lindblom and Habermas and also the issue that has perennially divided U.S. political parties. Although the views of Lindblom and Habermas are not the common currency of U.S. politics, they provide insight into how this question might be addressed.

Lindblom and Habermas both conclude that political controls over the economy affect the extent to which societies remain or become free and democratic, but they disagree about what types of controls have what effects. The Lindblomian thesis is that current interventions in the economy limit the range of issues raised in the political system because they leave business leaders in control of the level of production. In turn, the narrow scope of issues in politics constrains volitions in the public. Conversely, Habermas believes that current policies have already placed new responsibilities on the government and raised new issues, but he argues that the system's legitimating ideology, which claims incorrectly that the economy equitably and efficiently allocates consumable values, precludes direct control of investment and makes it impossible for the state to achieve the objectives that it sets for itself. From the latter perspective, which is based on Habermas's premise that the sociocultural system is principled, the effect of existing policies is to generate expectations that cannot be satisfied. Thus, where Lindblom sees a modest amount of circularity and constrained volitions, Habermas sees as a syndrome a set of crises culminating in motivation problems among the population.

To address these and similar issues, policy analysts will have to turn to methodologies in political science. Two domains of inquiry are particularly important. First, attention needs to be paid to public opinion, not the public opinion examined in marketing studies and opinion polls, but the opinions hypothesized in conflicting social and political theories. To begin with, it would be useful to investigate circularity, anomie, and alienation. Rather than researching how public opinion affects policy, we need to examine the effects of policy on public opinion in this broader sense.

Second, the reactions of policy makers and the public to the research itself should be examined. Much of the literature on the methodology of policy research, and much of the argument over public policy, centers on questions of political practicality. Policy analysis could perform a valuable public service by assessing the responsiveness of the political system and by identifying key segments of the population who can be motivated to take desirable political action. At this point, we do not know whom to address with our research. Should it be the public conscience, or the public's perceptions of costs and benefits, or top leaders in government, or the new social movements? How policy research itself affects politics has substantive implications for political theory and methodological implications for policy analysis.

Conclusion

Was the Great Society a valuable contribution to equality, or instead a misguided initiative that did more harm than good? It all depends on how you look at it. At this point in both politics and social science, we have far too much partisan speculation and not nearly enough critical analysis to reach a conclusion. The source of our confusion is a methodology of policy research that produces evidence devoid of clear theoretical implications. The facts confront us like pebbles in a kaleidoscope, capable of being rearranged and reinterpreted with each twist of the theoretical lens. It is time to discard this fruitless approach to policy evaluation and to explore alternatives grounded in comprehensive social and political theory.

Notes

Chapter 1

1. There are several kinds of policy research. For a typology, see deHaven-Smith and Ripley (1984). In large part I am concerned with the experimental model of program evaluation. For a detailed description of this model, see Houston (1972) and Weiss (1972). The experimental model (along with quasi-experimental versions of it) is by far the most common approach to policy research. It is also a prerequisite for such standard analytic techniques as cost-benefit analysis and cost-effectiveness analysis. Additionally, a focus on program performance narrowly conceived is characteristic of nonexperimental research designs, including (1) social audits, which trace the distribution of program resources from their point of origin to their intended recipients; (2) tracking studies, which track the flow of program participants from their point of program entry to their termination from the program; and (3) implementation studies or formative evaluations, which examine the administrative changes that occur in an agency as a program is carried out.
2. Lindblom (1983, p. 384) has suggested that he should no longer be referred to as a pluralist. In placing him within the pluralist tradition, I do not mean to imply that he adheres to a simplistic, group politics model. I believe that he has reformulated pluralism to take into account that the "pluralness" of group politics in any given society depends on the structure of the society's economy. If Lindblom is a pluralist, then pluralism has absorbed some of the key insights of Marxism.
3. In 1960, 21.2 percent of the poverty population was composed of persons under sixty-five living in female-headed households. By 1970, the figure had risen to 34 percent, and by 1980 it was at 42.2 percent. See U.S. Department of Commerce, Bureau of the Census, *Money Income and Poverty Status of Families and Persons in the United States: 1982*, Current Population Report, Series P-60, no. 140, Table 15.

Chapter 2

1. This is not to say that the social scientists in economics, sociology, and political science had reached a consensus and simply transmitted their

theories to policy makers. To the contrary, the social sciences are, and were in the 1960s, characterized by theoretical pluralism. When Truman (1951) was developing group theory, C. Wright Mills was proposing his version of elitism, and Friedman (1962) was laying out monetarism and other components of the conservative credo. In developing policy frameworks, policy makers pick and choose, more or less arbitrarily, among a range of conflicting theories and disciplinary orientations. As Wilson (1981) has shown, the research supporting many of the ideas drawn on to develop the Great Society was skimpy to the extreme.

2. It is impossible to say exactly how much was spent on the Great Society. The approach used by Murray (1984) is to include all social welfare expenditures. In contrast, Aaron (1978) differentiates between expenditures that were exclusively for the poor and expenditures that went partly for the middle class. As we shall see in chapter 6, the tendency of policy makers to expand income transfers and to shift benefits from the Great Society to the middle class has significant theoretical import.

Year	Total social welfare expenditures (*in millions*)	Spent exclusively on poor (*in millions*)	Total U.S. population (*in thousands*)	Persons in poverty (*in thousands*)
1965	98,277	6,136	193,526	33,185
1966	115,010	n/a	195,576	28,510
1967	131,200	10,637	197,457	27,769
1968	142,614	n/a	199,399	25,389
1969	153,378	14,489	201,385	24,147
1970	163,822	n/a	203,810	25,420
1971	287,911	22,972	206,212	25,559
1972	209,246	n/a	208,230	24,460
1973	227,021	27,625	209,851	22,973
1974	229,104	n/a	211,390	23,370
1975	256,104	31,491	213,137	25,877
1976	285,412	34,466	214,680	24,975
1977	296,411	n/a	216,400	24,720
1978	302,813	n/a	218,228	24,497
1979	299,976	n/a	220,099	26,072
1980	303,345	n/a	226,505	29,272

The data listed in the above table on social welfare expenditures, U.S. population, and persons in poverty are from Murray (1984, pp. 241–42, 245). Data on expenditures exclusively on the poor are from Aaron

(1978). Murray's expenditure data are in 1980 dollars. Aaron's expenditure figures are not adjusted for inflation. Murray's figures are used to reach the $3.5 trillion total cited in the text. Aaron's figures, if averaged for the period 1965–80 and put in 1980 dollars, would total $618 billion.

3. There were two views among policy makers about the role that CAAs were supposed to play. One perspective was that CAAs should mobilize the poor politically. The other viewpoint envisioned CAAs as a mechanism for outreach to the poor (who, because of their presumed alienation, would not have been expected to participate in social action programs without some unique delivery system) and as an organizational form for concentrating a variety of benefits on individual neighborhoods. This disagreement over the role of CAAs is discussed in Moynihan (1969).

4. The initial thrust of the Great Society of using in-kind transfers and social action programs was overlaid in the 1970s with an emphasis on cash transfers. We will examine this twist in the evolution of antipoverty policy in chapter 6.

5. The 1964 *Economic Report of the President* (p. 77) made this quite clear: "Conquest of poverty is well within our power. About $11 billion a year would bring all poor families up to the $3,000 income level we have taken to be the minimum of a decent life. The majority of the nation could simply tax themselves enough to provide the necessary income supplements to their less fortunate citizens. The burden—one fifth of the annual defense budget, less than 2 percent of GNP—would certainly not be intolerable. But this 'solution' would leave untouched most of the roots of poverty. Americans want to *earn* the American standard of living by their own efforts and contributions. It will be far better, even if more difficult, to equip and to permit the poor of the nation to produce and to earn the additional $11 billion, and more. We can surely afford greater generosity in relief of distress. But the major thrust of our campaign must be against causes rather than symptoms. We can afford the cost of that campaign too."

6. In 1980, the poverty threshold was $6,539 for a family of three persons, and $8,385 for a family of four. See Rodgers (1982, p. 17) for a table on thresholds for families of other sizes.

7. Levitan and Taggart (1976, pp. 71–72) summarize a 1972 report from the General Accounting Office showing that of those recipients who received one benefit, two-thirds participated in two or more programs and almost one-fifth participated in five or more.

8. The following table shows the incidence of poverty in the United States, 1965–80. Data are from the *Statistical Abstract of the United States*, various years.

Year	U.S. population (in thousands)	Persons in poverty (in thousands)	Incidence of poverty (percentage)
1965	193,526	33,185	17
1966	195,576	28,510	14
1967	197,457	27,769	14
1968	199,399	25,389	12
1969	201,385	24,147	11
1970	203,810	25,420	12
1971	206,212	25,559	12
1972	208,230	24,460	11
1973	209,851	22,973	10
1974	211,390	23,370	11
1975	213,137	25,877	12
1976	214,680	24,975	11
1977	216,400	24,720	11
1978	218,228	24,497	11
1979	220,099	26,072	11
1980	226,505	29,272	12

Chapter 3

1. A clear statement of this thesis is made by Sawhill (1986, p. 91): "Many now believe that government's commitment to provide full employment and a modicum of economic security has made it more difficult to keep inflation in check and to insure maximum work and thrift among the nation's citizens. In addition, memories of depression and of extreme poverty have faded as an older generation has passed on, and a younger one, born into prosperity, has begun to take its economic security for granted. Finally, the poor performance of the economy left many people dissatisfied. For all these reasons the stage was set in 1980 for the pendulum, which had been swinging leftward since the 1930s, to swing back again as part of what many would call the Reagan revolution."
2. One of the largest cuts was in Aid to Families with Dependent Children (AFDC), the bulk of which goes to poor females. Changes in AFDC eligibility criteria introduced under the Omnibus Budget Reconciliation Act (OBRA) of 1981 were designed to focus benefits on individuals without other sources of income. The changes appear to have had this effect (Nathan and Doolittle, 1984).

3. In *Politics and the Professors,* Aaron never explicitly states his own conception of poverty, but the way he analyzes the Great Society suggests
   that he sees poverty as a temporary state caused primarily by economic
   conditions. Except for the supposedly small group that stays poor all of
   the time, those who fall into poverty, Aaron implies, simply had a run of
   bad luck. This viewpoint leads Aaron to pay very little attention to the
   Negative Income Tax experiments and to the findings from compensatory
   education indicating that the poor have low levels of intelligence and
   ability. It also leads him to misinterpret the report from the Panel Study
   on Income Dynamics. He completely ignores (see Aaron, p. 36) the finding from the study that a threshold 50 percent above the poverty line
   yields a stable poverty population (see Lane and Morgan, 1975, p. 35).
   This is simply another example of how theoretical presuppositions, no
   matter how poorly articulated or unconscious, shape an analyst's interpretations of program performance.

Chapter 4

1. Liberal democracy is defined as a political-economic system that has
   competitive elections, constitutionally protected liberties, and a capitalist
   economy. In contrast, socialism involves extensive public ownership of
   corporations.
2. Unless otherwise noted, page numbers refer to Lindblom (1977).
3. See p. 98. Lindblom argues that planner sovereignty can be extended over
   both consumer and labor markets. In consumer markets, the government
   could purchase all consumer goods and then make them available to consumers either by allocating them, as in wartime rationing, or by selling
   them. Although Lindblom does not say so directly, he suggests that this
   form of intervention into the economy would extricate polyarchies from
   their recurring fiscal crises, since under planner sovereignty the polyarchies could steer their economies without deficit spending.

   In labor markets, planner sovereignty could operate in the same way.
   Governments could, in effect, hire all wage earners and then charge producers adjusted wage rates when producers hire labor from the government. Lindblom pays scant attention to labor market planner sovereignty
   because, I think, he does not see it as politically practical in the polyarchies.

   It should be noted that Lindblom's strategy for steering the economy
   through planner sovereignty corresponds to his view of how markets
   coordinate production—they set relative values for inputs in such a way
   that production responds to consumer preferences. The problem encountered by communist systems, Lindblom says, is in trying to accom-

plish this by setting input prices or quotas in intermediate markets. To avoid this problem, Lindblom prescribes planner sovereignty, which replaces the consumer as sovereign but allows input prices to be set freely in intermediate markets.

4. See pp. 349–50. Lindblom says, "One can of course imagine a broad public indisposition to indulge the corporation with financial benefits designed to compensate them for accepting a reduction of their freedom of action. Why, it might be asked, must the government and the public pay for the privilege of imposing controls the imposition of which presumably lies within the authority of government? But it is not a question of rights or authority. It is a practical question of combining social control over business enterprises with inducements for business."

5. See p. 346. Lindblom calls this type of planning "strategic" as opposed to "synoptic." Synoptic planning, which Lindblom associates with the synoptic theory advocated by socialists, is a form of ends-means analysis requiring, Lindblom argues, that all alternative means for achieving a given end be known in advance of planning. Recall that this was Lindblom's argument in "The Science of 'Muddling Through'." Given Lindblom's epistemological agnosticism—his belief that the human intellect has a limited capacity—he suggests that attempts to plan synoptically will result in big mistakes. Hence he counsels strategic analysis, which can adapt analysis to interaction in three ways: (1) It can tell a participant in interaction, e.g., a citizen, interest group, or policy maker, "how he can play his interactive role better to get what he wants" (p. 316); (2) It can tell people how to enter existing interactions for the purpose of achieving some "public purpose"; and (3) It can identify "possible changes in the basic structure of interaction processes themselves" (p. 316). See pp. 313–29.

Chapter 5

1. There is a very clear statement of this view of human nature in Dahl and Lindblom's *Politics, Economics, and Welfare,* originally published in 1953 and re-released in 1976. The book discusses (p. 97) the individual's "subjective 'field' of awareness," that is, "each individual's own special conscious and unconscious awareness of the universe made up of the self and its relations with objects, resources and capacities, feelings of reward and deprivation, symbols and expectations." Looking at people in this way, Dahl and Lindblom go on to say (pp. 98–99), "one can control another person's field by acting on his information, signals, communications, cues, or symbols and thereby affecting his expectations about rewards or deprivations; or one can act on the rewards and deprivations

that actually operate on the subordinate, thereby affecting his expectations; or one can act on both." This same notion of a "subjective field of awareness" is implicit in Lindblom's account in *Politics and Markets* of mechanisms of social control.

2. Private Industry Councils (PICs) were first established by the Private Sector Initiatives Program under Title VII of the 1978 reauthorization of the Comprehensive Employment and Training Act (CETA). Until 1982 they handled only a very small part of the CETA budget. When the Job Training Partnership Act replaced CETA in 1982, PICs were given a much larger role. For a summary of PSIP, see Ripley and Franklin (1986), pp. 17–19, 193–94.

Chapter 6

1. For Habermas's epistemology and his views on modern science, see *Knowledge and Human Interest*. For an overview of Habermas's works, as well as for some citations of works that have yet to be translated into English, see McCarthy (1978).
2. The transition to modernity is treated most extensively in *The Theory of Communicative Action*. Other historical shifts are addressed most fully in *Legitimation Crisis* and *Communication and the Evolution of Society*.
3. See Habermas, "Toward a Reconstruction of Historical Materialism," p. 157. In this essay, as well as in "Historical Materialism and the Development of Normative Structures," Habermas has clarified and elaborated the view of primitive and traditional societies sketched in *Legitimation Crisis*. In order to make his position somewhat more comprehensible, occasionally I have drawn on this material in presenting Habermas's account of social evolution in *Legitimation Crisis*.
4. Habermas does not analyze socialist societies, but he does suggest that they are very similar to organized capitalist societies in that they organize science for the purpose of increasing production, they have "an elitist disposition of the means of production," and they legitimate the state with a technocratic version of Marxism (see *Legitimation Crisis*, p. 3).
5. This account of the transition to traditional society is from Habermas, "Toward a Reconstruction of Historical Materialism," pp. 158–64.

Chapter 7

1. Management in the monopolistic and public sectors benefits from a large competitive sector with low wages because low wages in the competitive sector and the availability of a large pool of unorganized labor keep the wage demands of workers in the public and monopolistic sectors at acceptable levels. For their part, workers in the latter sectors favor a large

competitive sector because the scarcity of skilled jobs, and their organized monopoly over access to these jobs, keeps their wages relatively high. Consequently, "there is a convergence of the middle-range demands" of both organized labor and monopoly capital on the state, demands that call for public works, armaments production, space travel, and education for enhancing the skills of the labor force.

2. Habermas's argument that capitalism is stabilized in a sort of psychological cement comes from some of the early work of the Frankfurt School. See, especially, Adorno et al. (1950). In effect, the argument seeks to relativize Freud's description of the psyche. Freud viewed the superego as particularly rigid and repressive, but he lacked a theory of ethics that would have allowed him to conceptualize the superego as amenable to flexibility and criticism. Hence he concluded that its rigidity was rooted in the human condition. In contrast, Habermas's argument is that the superego described by Freud is the superego developed in capitalism.

3. Several other authors have noted this phenomenon. See Murray (1984, pp. 45–57) and Aaron (1978, pp. 4–15).

4. The transformation of the Great Society occurred in large part under the Nixon administration. During his successful campaign for the presidency in 1968, Nixon said that welfare should be provided only to those who cannot help themselves, whereas others should be given incentives "to move off welfare rolls and onto private payrolls" (Moynihan, 1973, p. 67). Once in office, however, Nixon proposed a Family Assistance Program (FAP) that in reality was a guaranteed income. Every family was to be assured an annual income of at least $1,600. The Family Assistance Program was never enacted into law—it failed in the Senate—but it exemplified the way in which the Great Society was transformed from an effort to enhance the capabilities of the poor into a massive and yet disguised scheme for propping up incomes.

How did President Nixon make his proposal for a guaranteed income square with the philosophy of free markets and individual initiative that he espoused during the campaign? He consciously misled the public into believing that the Family Assistant Program was a scheme for promoting work. Like the "thirty dollars plus one-third rule" under AFDC, the Family Assistance Program allowed workers to keep part of their income without losing the FAP subsidy, and for those workers who refused to work or to participate in training, it reduced the income guarantee by $300. Hence, publicly Nixon argued that the work requirement in FAP meant that the program was more conducive to labor force entry than standard welfare. Privately, however, he said: "I don't care a damn about a work requirement. This is the price of getting the $1,600" (Moynihan,

1973, pp. 219–20). In short, a guaranteed income was concealed within the Trojan horse of welfare reform.

5. For example, the 1970 Food Stamp Reform Act required registration for and acceptance of jobs by able-bodied adults as a prerequisite for food aid (Sobel, 1977, p. 94). This requirement is similar to the one under unemployment insurance, where recipients must show that they are actively seeking employment while they receive benefits. Such requirements are virtually impossible to enforce. Participants can fake looking for work, can behave so badly on interviews that employers refuse to hire them, and so on.

6. The $4 billion figure in this sentence and the $13 billion figure in the next sentence include jobs programs in addition to CETA public service employment (PSE). Nevertheless, it is fair to say that PSE programs dominated CETA almost from its inception. They attracted the most attention from local elected officials, often involved major efforts to locate enough enrollees for expending all the available funds, and, after the 1978 CETA reforms, were very difficult to administer.

7. This means that the grants economy employs about one-fourth of all the service workers in the nation and accounts for about 5 percent of the gross domestic product (Salamon, 1984, p. 264).

8. The three-sector model can also account for the finding that the earnings of new entrants into the labor force evidence a sustained increase after employment programs. All that is required is an auxiliary hypothesis that workers' orientation to work is commensurate with their opportunities. Workers in the competitive sector have a weak attachment to the labor force (and hence experience low wages and periodic employment) because there is no reason for them to have a strong attachment. The only jobs that they can obtain pay low wages, have high turnover, and offer little opportunity for advancement. Given the situation, it makes sense to work a while and then take some time off, because the worker can always get a similar job whenever he wants. Participants in training programs might have shown wage gains initially because they stayed on the job longer after training on the basis of a mistaken belief that they were on a path to improved earnings. However, once they realized that they were in another dead-end job, they returned to normal work patterns in the lower class. Similarly, new entrants into the labor force might have experienced longer lasting wage gains because it took them longer to realize that they were on a course with a dead end. This is a testable hypothesis; the expectation is that the wage gains of new entrants into the labor force would have dissipated. Unfortunately, the impact evaluations in employment and training programs had a short duration, so there is no way of testing the hypothesis with available data.

9. Even when responses are not restricted just to those who say they have "a
   great deal" of confidence in the institutions, but also include the "quite a
   lot" category (as opposed to "some," "very little," and "none"), confidence in American institutions remains low. In 1985, Congress, news-
   papers, big business, television, and organized labor all received support
   from less than 40 percent of the public. See *The Gallup Report*, Report
   No. 238, July 1985.

References

Aaron, Henry J. (1978). *Politics and the Professors: The Great Society in Perspective.* Washington: The Brookings Institution.

Action, J. P. (1973). *Evaluating Public Programs to Save Lives: The Case of Heart Attacks.* R-950-RC. Santa Monica, CA: The Rand Corporation.

Anderson, Charles W. (1978). "The Political Economy of Charles E. Lindblom." *American Political Science Review* 72(3): 1012–16.

_____. (1979). "The Place of Principles in Policy Analysis." *American Political Science Review* 73: 711–23.

Anderson, Martin (1978). *Welfare.* Stanford, CA: Hoover Institution Press.

Archibald, K. A. (1970). "Three Views of the Expert's Role in Policy Making: Systems Analysis, Incrementalism, and the Clinical Approach." *Policy Sciences* 1: 73–86.

Ashenfelter, Orley, and Heckman, James (1973). "Changes in Minority Employment Patterns." Prepared for the Equal Opportunity Commission. Mimeographed.

Bachrach, Peter, and Baratz, Morton S. (1962). "Two Faces of Power." *American Political Science Review* 56: 947–52.

Bardach, Eugene (1977). *The Implementation Game: What Happens after a Bill Becomes a Law.* Cambridge, MA: MIT Press.

Baumer, Donald C., and Van Horn, Carl E. (1985). *The Politics of Unemployment.* Washington: Congressional Quarterly Press.

Bawden, D. Lee, and Palmer, John L. (1984). "Social Policy: Challenging the Welfare State." In Palmer and Sawhill, eds., *The Reagan Record,* q.v.

Beltrami, E. J. (1977). *Models for Public Systems Analysis.* London: Academic Press.

Berger, Peter L. (1986). *The Capitalist Revolution: Fifty Propositions About Prosperity, Equality, and Liberty.* New York: Basic Books.

Berman, Paul (1978). "The Study of Macro and Micro Implementation." *Public Policy* 26(2): 157–84.

Bernstein, Richard J. (1976). *The Restructuring of Social and Political Theory.* New York: Harcourt Brace.

Berrueta-Clement, John R., et al. (1984). *Changed Lives: The Effects of the Perry Preschool Program on Youths Through Age 19.* Ypsilanti, MI: High/Scope Press.

Bishop, John H. (1980). "Jobs, Cash Transfers, and Marital Instability: A Review and Synthesis of the Evidence." *Journal of Human Resources* 15: 301–34.

Blumstein, Alfred (1971). "Cost Effectiveness Analysis in the Allocation of Policy Resources." In *Cost Benefit Analysis* edited by M. G. Kendall. London: English Universities Press, pp. 87–88.

Boeckmann, M. E. (1976). "Policy Impacts of the New Jersey Income Maintenance Experiment." *Policy Sciences* 7(1): 53–76.

Borus, Michael E. (1979). *Measuring the Impact of Employment-Related Social Programs*. Kalamazoo, MI: W. E. Upjohn Institute for Employment Research.

Boulding, Kenneth E. (1973). *The Economy of Love and Fear: A Preface to Grants Economics*. Belmont, CA: Wadsworth.

Bowles, Samuel, and Gintis, Herbert (1986). *Democracy and Capitalism: Property, Community, and the Contradictions of Modern Social Thought*. New York: Basic Books.

Braybrooke, David, and Lindblom, Charles E. (1963, 1970). *A Strategy of Decision: Policy Evaluation as a Social Process*. New York: The Free Press.

Brecher, Charles (1973). *The Impact of Federal Antipoverty Policies*. New York: Praeger Publishers.

Brewer, Gary D., and deLeon, Peter (1983). *The Foundations of Policy Analysis*. Homewood, IL: Dorsey.

Brown, Peter G. (1976). "Ethics and Policy Research." *Policy Analysis* 1: 325–40.

Burstein, Paul (1979). "Public Opinion, Demonstrations, and the Passage of Antidiscrimination Legislation." *Public Opinion Quarterly* 43: 157–72.

Cain, Glen G., and Watts, Harold W. (1972). "Problems in Making Policy Inferences from the Coleman Report." In Rossi and Williams, eds., q.v., pp. 73–95.

Campbell, Donald T., and Stanley, Julian C. (1963). *Experimental and Quasi-Experimental Designs for Research*. Chicago: Rand McNally.

Carter, Reginald K. (1971). "Clients' Resistance to Negative Findings and the Latent Conservative Function of Evaluation Studies." *American Sociologist* 6: 118–24.

Cater, Douglass (1964). *Power in Washington*. New York: Random House.

Champlin, John R. (1979). "Lie Back and Enjoy It: Remarks on the Unavoidability of Theory." Mimeo presented at The Interpretive Act: Theory and Practice, An Interdisciplinary Symposium on Contemporary Critical Theory, sponsored by the Division of Comparative Studies, The Ohio State University, April 18–19.

Cicirelli, Victor G., et al. (1969). *The Impact of Head Start: An Evaluation of the Effect of Head Start on Children's Cognitive and Affective Development*. Report presented to the Office of Economic Opportunity by Westinghouse Learning Corporation, Ohio University.

Coker, Francis W. (1921). "The Technique of the Pluralist State." *American Political Science Review* 15: 186–213.

Coleman, James S. (1972). *Policy Research in The Social Sciences*. Morristown, NJ.: General Learning Press.

Coleman, James S.; Campbell, Ernest Q.; Hobson, Carol J.; McPartland, James; Mood, Alexander M.; Weinfeld, Frederic D.; and York, Robert L. (1966). *Equality of Educational Opportunity*. Washington: U.S. Government Printing Office.

Committee for Economic Development (1970). *Further Weapons against Inflation*. New York: CED.

_____. (1972). *High Employment without Inflation*. New York: CED.

_____. (1976). *Fighting Inflation and Promoting Growth*. New York: CED.

Condran, John G. (1979). "Changes in White Attitudes Toward Blacks: 1963–1977." *Public Opinion Quarterly* (Winter): 463–76.

Cumming, Robert Denoon (1969). *Human Nature and History: A Study of the Development of Liberal Political Thought*. Chicago: University of Chicago Press.

Dahl, Robert A. (1956). *A Preface to Democratic Theory*. Chicago: University of Chicago Press.

_____. (1982). *Dilemmas of Pluralist Democracy: Autonomy vs. Control*. New Haven: Yale University Press.

Dahl, Robert A., and Lindblom, Charles E. (1953). *Politics, Economics, and Welfare*. Chicago: University of Chicago Press.

Dahrendorf, Ralf (1959). *Class and Class Conflict in Industrial Society*. Stanford, CA: Stanford University Press.

Davis, Dwight F., and Portis, Edward B. (1982). "A Categorical Imperative for Social Scientific Policy Evaluation." *Administration and Society* 14: 175–94.

deHaven-Smith, Lance (1983). "Evidence on the Minimal Management Principle of Program Design: Implementation of the Targeted Jobs Tax Credit." *Journal of Politics* 45: 711–30.

deHaven-Smith, Lance, and Ripley, Randall B. (1984). "The Political-Theoretic Foundations of Public Policy." Paper presented at the Southwest Political Science Association Annual Convention in Fort Worth, Texas.

deHaven-Smith, Lance, and Van Horn, Carl E. (1984). "Subgovernment Conflict in Public Policy." *Policy Studies Journal* 12: 627–42.

Derthick, Martha (1972). *New Towns In-Town*. Washington: The Urban Institute.

Dewey, John (1927). *The Public and Its Problems*. Chicago: The Swallow Press, Inc.

Doeringer, Peter B., and Piore, Michael J. (1971). *Internal Labor Markets and Manpower Analysis*. Lexington, MA: D.C. Heath and Company.

Dorfman, Robert (1965). *Measuring Benefits of Government Investments*. Washington: Brookings Institution.

Ellis, Ellen Deborah (1920). "The Pluralistic State." *American Political Science Review* 19: 393–407.

Feldman, Elliot J. (1976). "An Antidote for Apology, Service and Witchcraft in Policy Analysis." In *Problems of Theory in Policy Analysis*, edited by Phillip M. Gregg. Lexington, MA: Lexington Books, pp. 19–27.

Feyerabend, Paul (1970). "Consolations for the Specialist." In Lakatos and Musgrave, eds., pp. 197–231, q.v.

Fischer, Frank (1980). *Politics, Values, and Public Policy*. Boulder, CO: Westview Press.

Flood, Tony (1977–78). "Jürgen Habermas's Critique of Marxism." *Science and Society* 41(4): 448–64.

Foucault, Michel (1965). *Madness and Civilization: A History of Insanity in the Age of Reason*. Translated by Richard Howard. New York: Random House.

———. (1978). *The History of Sexuality*. Translated by Robert Hurley. New York: Random House.

Freeman, J. Leiper (1955). *The Political Process*. New York: Random House.

Friedman, Lawrence M. (1977). "The Social and Political Context of the War on Poverty: An Overview." In Haveman, ed., pp. 21–47, q.v.

Friedman, Milton (1962). *Capitalism and Freedom*. Chicago: University of Chicago Press.

Gans, Herbert J. (1971). "Social Science for Social Policy." In *The Use and Abuse of Social Science*, edited by Irving Louis Horowitz. New Brunswick, NJ.: Transaction Books.

Gewirth, Alan (1960). "Positive 'Ethics' and 'Normative Science'." *Philosophical Review* 69: 311–30.

Gilder, George (1981). *Wealth and Poverty*. New York: Basic Books.

———. (1983). "A Supply-Side Economics of the Left." *The Public Interest* 72: 29–43.

Gilpin, Robert (1964). "Natural Scientists in Policy Making." In *Scientists and National Policy-Making*, edited by Robert Gilpin and Christopher Wright. New York: Columbia University Press, pp. 1–18.

Glennan, Thomas K., Jr. (1972). "Evaluating Federal Manpower Programs: Notes and Observations." In Rossi and Williams, eds., q.v.

Goldstein, Richard, and Sachs, Stephen M., eds. (1984). *Applied Poverty Research*. Totowa, NJ: Rowman & Allanheld.

Goodwin, Leonard (1972). *Do the Poor Want to Work?* Washington: The Brookings Institution.

Gordon, David M. (1972). *Theories of Poverty and Unemployment.* Lexington, MA: Lexington Books.

Greeley, Andrew M., and Sheatsley, Paul B. (1971). "Attitudes toward Racial Integration." *Scientific American* 225(6): 13–19.

Habermas, Jürgen (1968, 1971). *Knowledge and Human Interests.* Translated by Jeremy J. Shapiro. Boston: Beacon Press.

_____. (1970). *Toward a Rational Society.* Translated by Jeremy J. Shapiro. Boston: Beacon Press.

_____. (1973). *Theory and Practice.* Translated by John Viertzel. Boston: Beacon Press.

_____. (1973, 1975). *Legitimation Crisis.* Translated by Thomas McCarthy. Boston: Beacon Press.

_____. (1976). "Toward a Reconstruction of Historical Materialism." In *Communication and the Evolution of Society,* translated by Thomas McCarthy. Boston: Beacon Press, pp. 95–129.

_____. (1980). *Communication and the Evolution of Society.* Translated by Thomas McCarthy. Boston: Beacon Press.

_____. (1981). *The Theory of Communicative Action,* vol. 1: *Reason and the Rationalization of Society.* Translated by Thomas McCarthy. Boston: Beacon Press.

Hargrove, F. (1975). *The Missing Link: The Study of Implementation of Social Policy.* Washington: The Urban Institute.

Harrington, Michael (1984). *The New American Poverty.* New York: Penguin Books.

Haveman, Robert H. (1977). "Introduction: Poverty and Social Policy in the 1960s and 1970s—An Overview and Some Speculations." In Haveman, ed., pp. 1–20, q.v.

_____, ed. (1977). *A Decade of Federal Antipoverty Programs.* New York: Academic Press.

Heather, Gerard P. and Stolz, Matthew (1979). "Hanna Arendt and the Problem of Critical Theory." *Journal of Politics* 41:2–22.

Heclo, Hugh (1978). "Issue Networks and the Executive Establishment." In *The New American Political System,* edited by Anthony King. Washington: American Enterprise Institute for Public Policy Research.

_____. (1986). "Reaganism and the Search for a Public Philosophy." In *Perspectives on the Reagan Years,* edited by John L. Palmer. Washington: The Urban Institute Press.

Hill, Melvyn A. (1972). "Jürgen Habermas: A Social Science of the Mind." *Philosophy of Social Science* 2:247–56.

Hirschman, Albert O. (1982). *Shifting Involvements: Private Interests, Public Action.* Princeton: Princeton University Press.

Horowitz, Irving Louis (1970). "Social Science Mandarins: Policymaking as a Political Formula." *Policy Sciences* 1: 339–60.

Houston, Tom R., Jr. (1972). "The Behavioral Sciences Impact-Effectiveness Model." In Rossi and Williams, eds., pp. 42–66, q.v.

Hyman, Herbert H., and Sheatsley, Paul B. (1984). "Attitudes toward Desegregation." *Scientific American* 211(1): 16–23.

Jantsch, Erich (1970). "From Forecasting and Planning to Policy Sciences." *Policy Sciences* 1: 31–47.

Jay, Martin (1973). *The Dialectical Imagination.* Boston: Beacon Press.

Jencks, Christopher, et al. (1972). *Inequality: A Reassessment of the Effect of Family and Schooling in America.* New York: Basic Books, Inc.

Jones, Charles O. (1977, 1984). *An Introduction to the Study of Public Policy.* Monterey, CA: Brooks/Cole.

Kaplan, Abraham (1964). *The Conduct of Inquiry.* San Francisco: Chandler Books.

Kaplan, Marshall, and Cuciti, Peggy L., eds. (1986). *The Great Society and Its Legacy: Twenty Years of U.S. Public Policy.* Durham, NC: Duke University Press.

Katz, Michael B. (1986). *In the Shadow of the Poorhouse: A Social History of Welfare in America.* New York: Basic Books.

Keat, Russell (1981). *The Politics of Social Theory: Habermas, Freud, and the Critique of Positivism.* Chicago: University of Chicago Press.

Kershaw, Joseph H., and Levine, Robert (1966). "Poverty, Aggregate Demand, and Economic Structure." *Journal of Human Resources* 1: 66–80.

Key, V. O., Jr. (1942). *Politics, Parties, and Pressure Groups.* New York: Thomas Y. Crowell.

Kinder, Donald R., and Rhodebeck, Laurie A. (1982). "Continuities in Support for Racial Equality, 1972 to 1976." *Public Opinion Quarterly* 46: 195–215.

Kuhn, Thomas S. (1962). *The Structure of Scientific Revolutions.* Chicago: University of Chicago Press.

Ladd, Everett Carll (1976–77). "The Polls: The Question of Confidence." *Public Opinion Quarterly* (Winter): 544–52.

Laffer, Arthur B., and Seymour, Jan B. (1979). *The Economics of the Tax Revolt.* New York: Harcourt Brace Jovanovich, Inc.

Lakatos, Imre (1970). "Falsification and the Methodology of Scientific Research Programmes." In Lakatos and Musgrave, eds., pp. 91–196, q.v.

Lakatos, Imre, and Musgrave, Alan, eds. (1970). *Criticism and the Growth of Knowledge.* London: Cambridge University Press.

Lampman, Robert J. (1965). "Approaches to the Reduction of Poverty." *American Economic Review* 55:521–29.

Lane, Jonathan P., and Morgan, James N. (1975). "Patterns of Change in Economic Status and Family Structure." In *Five Thousand American Families—Patterns of Economic Progress: Analyses of the First Six Years of the Panel Study on Income Dynamics,* vol. 3, edited by Greg J. Duncan and James N. Morgan. Ann Arbor: Institute for Social Research, University of Michigan.

Lasswell, Harold D. (1951). "The Policy Orientation." In *The Policy Sciences,* edited by Daniel Lerner and Harold D. Lasswell. Stanford, CA: Stanford University Press.

Levin, Henry M. (1977). "A Decade of Policy Developments in Improving Education and Training for Low-Income Populations." In Haveman, ed., pp. 123–88, q.v.

Levine, Robert A. (1970). *The Poor Ye Need Not Have With You.* Cambridge, MA: The MIT Press.

Levitan, Sar A. (1973). *Programs in Aid of the Poor.* Baltimore: The Johns Hopkins University Press.

Levitan, Sar A., and Taggart, Robert (1976). *The Promise of Greatness.* Cambridge, MA: Harvard University Press.

Lewis, Oscar (1968). *The Study of Slum Culture—Backgrounds for La Vida.* New York: Random House.

Lindblom, Charles E. (1959). "The Science of 'Muddling Through'." *Public Administration Review* 19:79–88.

———. (1965). *The Intelligence of Democracy: Policy Making Through Mutual Adjustment.* New York: The Free Press.

———. (1968). *The Policy Making Process.* Englewood Cliffs, NJ: Prentice-Hall.

———. (1977). *Politics and Markets.* New York: Basic Books.

———. (1979). "Still Muddling, Not Yet Through." *The Public Administration Review* 39:517–27.

———. (1983). "Comment on Manley." *American Political Science Review* 77:384–86.

Lindblom, Charles E., and Cohen, David K. (1979). *Usable Knowledge.* New Haven: Yale University Press.

Lipset, Seymor Martin (1959). *Political Man.* New York: Anchor Books.

Lowi, Theodore J. (1969, 1979). *The End of Liberalism.* New York: Norton.

———. (1973). "What Political Scientists Don't Need to Ask about Policy Analysis." *Policy Studies Journal* 2:61–67.

Lynn, Laurence E., Jr. (1977). "A Decade of Policy Developments in the Income-Maintenance System." In Haveman, ed., pp. 55–117, q.v.

_____. (1980). *Designing Public Policy: A Casebook on the Role of Policy Analysis*. Santa Monica, CA: Goodyear Publishing Company.

McCarthy, Thomas (1978). *The Critical Theory of Jürgen Habermas*. Cambridge, MA: The MIT Press.

MacRae, Duncan, Jr. (1971). "Scientific Communication, Ethical Argument, and Public Policy." *American Political Science Review* 65: 38–50.

Manley, John F. (1983). "Neo-Pluralism: A Class Analysis of Pluralism I and Pluralism II." *American Political Science Review* 77: 368–84.

Marshall, Ray (1978). "A Message from the Secretary." In *Employment and Training Report of the President*. Washington: U.S. Government Printing Office, pp. 3–10.

Marx, Karl (1967). *Capital: A Critique of Political Economy*. New York: International Publishers.

_____. (1972, 1978). "Preface to a Contribution to the Critique of Political Economy." In *The Marx-Engels Reader*, edited by Robert C. Tucker. New York: W. W. Norton, and Co., Inc., pp. 3–6.

Miliband, Ralph (1969). *The State in Capitalist Society: An Analysis of the Western System of Power*. New York: Basic Books.

Mill, John Stuart (1965). *On the Logic of the Moral Sciences: A System of Logic*, Book IV. Indianapolis: Bobbs- Merrill.

Miller, Judith Droitcour, and Cisin, Ira H. (1983). *Highlights from the National Survey on Drug Abuse: 1982*. Washington: U.S. Government Printing Office.

Moffit, Robert A. (1981). "The Negative Income Tax: Would It Discourage Work?" *Monthly Labor Review* 57: 104–19.

Moynihan, Daniel P. (1968). "The Professors and the Poor." In *On Understanding Poverty*, edited by Daniel P. Moynihan. New York: Basic Books, Inc.

_____. (1969). *Maximum Feasible Misunderstanding: Community Action in the War on Poverty*. New York: The Free Press.

_____. (1973). *The Politics of a Guaranteed Income: The Nixon Administration and the Family Assistance Plan*. New York: Random House.

Murphy, Jerome (1971). "Title I of ESEA: The Politics of Implementing Federal Education Reform." *Harvard Educational Review* 41: 35–63.

Murray, Charles (1984). *Losing Ground: American Social Policy, 1950–1980*. New York: Manhattan Institute for Policy Research.

Natchez, Peter B. (1985). *Images of Voting/Visions of Democracy*. New York: Basic Books.

Nathan, Richard (1986). "Social Science and the Great Society." In Kaplan and Cuciti, eds., q.v.

Nathan, Richard P., and Doolittle, Fred C. (1984). "Overview: Effects of the Reagan Domestic Program on States and Localities." Paper presented at the Urban and Regional Research Center, Princeton University, 7 June.

National Commission for Employment Policy (1975). "Recent European Manpower Policy Initiatives." S.R. No. 3, November.

_____. (1975). "Proceedings for a Conference on the Role of the Business Sector in Manpower Policy." S.R. No. 4, November.

_____. (1976). "Proceedings of a Conference on Labor's Views on Manpower Policy." S.R. No. 6, February.

Nielsen, Victor G. (1975). "Why Evaluation Does Not Improve Program Effectiveness." *Policy Studies Journal* 3(4).

O'Connor, James (1978). *The Fiscal Crisis of the State*. New York: St. Martin's Press.

Offe, Claus (1984). *Contradictions of the Welfare State*. Edited and translated by John Keane. Cambridge: MIT Press.

Palmer, John L., and Sawhill, Isabel V. (1982). "Perspectives on the Reagan Experiment." In *The Reagan Experiment,* edited by John L. Palmer and Isabel V. Sawhill. Washington: The Urban Institute.

_____. (1984). *The Reagan Record*. Cambridge, MA: Ballinger Publishing Co.

Palumbo, Dennis J. (1981). "The State of Policy Studies Research and the Policy of the New *Policy Studies Review*." *Policy Studies Review* 1: 5–10.

Patton, Michael Q. (1978). *Utilization-Focused Evaluation*. Beverly Hills, CA: Sage Publications.

Pechman, Joseph A., and Timpane, P. Michael (1975). "Introduction and Summary." In *Work Incentives and Income Guarantees: The New Jersey Negative Income Tax Experiment,* edited by Joseph A. Pechman and P. Michael Timpane. Washington: The Brookings Institution, pp. 1–14.

Peterson, Paul E., and Greenstone, David J. (1977). "Racial Change and Citizen Participation: The Mobilization of Low-Income Communities Through Community Action." In Haveman, ed., pp. 241–78, q.v.

Plotnick, Robert D., and Skidmore, Felicity (1975). *Progress Against Poverty: A Review of the 1964–1974 Decade*. New York: Academic Press.

Popper, Karl R. (1944, 1962). *The Open Society and Its Enemies*. Princeton: Princeton University Press.

_____. (1959). *The Logic of Scientific Discovery*. New York: Basic Books.

Pressman, Jeffrey L., and Wildavsky, Aaron (1973). *Implementation*. Berkeley: University of California Press.

Preston, Larry M. (1984). "Freedom, Markets, and Voluntary Exchange." *American Political Science Review* 78: 959–70.

Rabinovitz, F., Pressman, J. Jr., and Rein, J. (1976). "Policy Implementation: Guidelines." *Policy Sciences* 7(4): 399–416.

Ravenal, Earl C. (1974). "Policy Relevance and Policy Models." *Policy Studies Journal* 2: 219–25.

Reagan, Michael D. (1969). *Science and the Federal Patron*. New York: Oxford University Press.

Reynolds, Morgan O. (1984). *Power and Privilege: Labor Unions in America*. New York: Universe Books.

Riecken, H. W., and Boruch, R. F., eds. (1974). *Social Experimentation: A Method for Planning and Evaluating Social Intervention*. New York: Academic Press.

Ripley, Randall B. (1977). "Policy Research and the Clinical Relationship." *Mershon Center Position Papers in the Policy Sciences*. Number 1.

_____. (1985). *Policy Analysis in Political Science*. Chicago: Nelson-Hall.

Ripley, Randall B., and Franklin, Grace A. (1980, 1984). *Congress, the Bureaucracy, and Public Policy*. Homewood, IL: Dorsey.

_____. (1982, 1986). *Policy Implementation and Bureaucracy*. Chicago: Dorsey.

Rivlin, Alice M. (1971). *Systematic Thinking for Social Action*. Washington: The Brookings Institution.

_____. (1974). *Social Policy: Alternate Strategies for the Federal Government*. Washington: The Brookings Institution. General Series Reprint 288.

Rodgers, Harrell R., Jr. (1982). *The Cost of Human Neglect*. Armonk, New York: M. E. Sharpe, Inc.

Rodgers, Harrell R., Jr., and Bullock, Charles S., III (1972). *Law and Social Change*. New York: McGraw-Hill.

Rose, Stephen M. (1972). *The Betrayal of the Poor: The Transformation of Community Action*. Cambridge, MA: Schenkman Publishing Company.

Rossi, Peter H. (1972). "Testing for Success and Failure in Social Action." In Rossi and Williams, eds., pp. 11–49, q.v.

Rossi, Peter H., and Williams, Walter, eds. (1972). *Evaluating Social Programs*. New York: Academic Press.

Salamon, Lester M. (1984). "Nonprofit Organizations: The Lost Opportunity." In Palmer and Sawhill, eds., *The Reagan Record*, pp. 261–86, q.v.

Sawhill, Isabel V. (1982). "Economic Policy." In Palmer and Sawhill, eds., *The Reagan Experiment*, 31–58, q.v.

_____. (1986). "Reaganomics in Retrospect." In *Perspectives on the Reagan Years*, edited by John L. Palmer. Washington: Urban Institute Press, pp. 91–120.

Schlesinger, Arthur M., Jr. (1957). *The Crisis of the Old Order*. Boston: Houghton Mifflin Company.

_____. (1959). *The Coming of the New Deal*. Boston: Houghton Mifflin Company.

_____. (1960). *The Politics of Upheaval*. Boston: Houghton Mifflin Company.

_____. (1986). *The Cycles of American History*. Boston: Houghton Mifflin Co.

Schultze, Charles L. (1968). *The Politics and Economics of Public Spending*. Washington: The Brookings Institution.

Schumpeter, Joseph A. (1976). *Capitalism, Socialism, and Democracy*. New York: Harper and Row.

Schwarz, John E. (1983). *America's Hidden Success: A Reassessment of Twenty Years of Public Policy*. New York: W.W. Norton.

Scriven, Michael (1967). "The Methodology of Evaluation." In *Perspectives of Curriculum Evaluation*, edited by Ralph W. Tyler, Robert M. Gagne, and Michael Scriven. AERA Monograph Series on Curriculum Evaluation, No. 1. Chicago: Rand McNally and Co., pp. 39–83.

Sheatsley, Paul B. (1966). "White Attitudes Toward the Negro." *Daedalus* (Winter): 217–38.

Sjoberg, Gideon (1975). "Politics, Ethics and Evaluation Research." In *Handbook of Evaluation Research*, edited by Marcia Guttentag and Elmer L. Struening. Beverly Hills: Sage Publications.

Skolnik, Alfred, and Dales, Sophie R. (1975). "Social Welfare Expenditures, Fiscal Year 1974." *Social Security Bulletin* (January).

Smeeding, Timothy M. (1975). "Measuring the Economic Welfare of Low Income Households and the Anti-Poverty Effectiveness of Cash and Non-Cash Transfer Programs." Ph.D. diss., University of Wisconsin, Madison.

Sobel, Lester A. (1977). *Welfare and the Poor*. New York: Facts on File, Inc.

Somit, Albert, and Tanenhaus, Joseph (1967). *The Development of Political Science: From Burgess to Behavioralism*. Boston: Allyn and Bacon.

Sowell, Thomas (1987). *A Conflict of Visions: Ideological Origins of Political Struggles*. New York: William Morrow and Co.

Sundquist, James L. (1968). *Politics and Policy: The Eisenhower, Kennedy, and Johnson Years*. Washington: The Brookings Institution.

Taylor, Charles (1973). "Neutrality in Political Science." In *The Philosophy of Social Explanation*, edited by Alan Ryan. London: Oxford University Press, pp. 139–70.

Theobold, Robert (1968). "The Guaranteed Income: What and Why." In *Issues of American Public Policy*, edited by John H. Bunzel. Englewood Cliffs, NJ: Prentice-Hall, Inc., pp. 99–107.

Toulmin, Stephen (1970). "Does the Distinction between Normal and Revolutionary Science Hold Water?" In Lakatos and Musgrave, eds., pp. 39–58, q.v.

Tribe, Laurence H.(1972). "Policy Science: Analysis or Ideology." In *Benefit-Cost and Policy Analysis 1972*. Chicago: Aldine Publishing Company, pp. 3–47.

Truman, David B. (1951). *The Governmental Process: Political Interests and Public Opinion*. New York: Alfred A. Knopf.

———. (1968). "The Social Sciences and Public Policy." *Science* 160: 508–12.

Ture, Norman B. (1980). *The Economic Effects of Tax Changes: A Neoclassical Analysis*. Washington: Institute for Research on the Economics of Taxation.

Van Horn, Carl E., and Van Meter, Donald J. (1974). "The Policy Implementation Process: A Conceptual Framework." *Administration of Society* 1: 445–88.

———. (1976). "The Implementation of Intergovernmental Policy." In *Public Policy Making in a Federal System*, edited by Charles O. Jones and Robert D. Thomas. Beverly Hills: Sage Publications, pp. 39–64.

Vogel, David (1987). "The New Political Science of Corporate Power." *The Public Interest* 87: 63–79.

Wallace, Phyllis A. (1977). "A Decade of Policy Developments in Equal Opportunity in Employment and Housing." In Haveman, ed., pp. 329–59, q.v.

Weber, Max (1947). *The Theory of Social and Economic Organization*. New York: Oxford University Press.

Weiss, Carol H. (1972). *Evaluation Research*. Englewood Cliffs, NJ: Prentice-Hall, Inc.

———. (1978). "Improving the Linkage Between Social Research and Public Policy." In *Knowledge and Policy: The Uncertain Connection*, edited by Laurence E. Lynn, Jr. Washington: National Academy of Sciences, pp. 23–81.

———. (1979). "The Many Meanings of Research Utilization." *Public Administration Review* 39: 426–31.

Westat, Inc. (1978). "Continuous Longitudinal Manpower Survey: Follow-up Report No. 1." Prepared for the Office of Program Evaluation, Employment and Training Administration, U.S. Dept. of Labor, July.

White, Stephen K. (1979). "Rationality and the Foundations of Political Philosophy: An Introduction to the Recent Work of Jürgen Habermas." *Journal of Politics* 41: 1156–71.

———. (1980). "Reason and Authority in Habermas: A Critique of the Critics." *American Political Science Review* 74: 1007–17.

———. (1986). "Foucault's Challenge to Critical Theory." *American Political Science Review* 80: 419–32.

Wildavsky, Aaron (1966). "The Political Economy of Efficiency: Cost-Benefit Analysis, Systems Analysis, and Program Budgeting." *Public Administration Review* 26(4): 292–310.

Williams, Alan (1972). "Cost-Benefit Analysis: Bastard Science? And/Or Insidious Poison in the Body Politic?" In *Benefit-Cost and Policy Analysis 1972*. Chicago: Aldine Publishing Company.

Wilson, James Q. (1981). "'Policy Intellectuals' and Public Policy." *The Public Interest* 64 (Summer): 31–46.

Index

151